Steps to Academic Reading 1

Steps and Plateaus

Second Edition

Jean Zukowski/Faust

Northern Arizona University

THOMSON
™
HEINLE

Australia • Canada • Mexico • Singapore • Spain • United Kingdom • United States

THOMSON
™
HEINLE

Steps to Academic Reading 1, Second Edition
Steps and Plateaus
Jean Zukowski/Faust

Developmental Editor: *Phyllis Dobbins*
Production Editor: *Angela Williams Urquhart*
Marketing Manager: *Katrina Byrd*
Manufacturing Coordinator: *Holly Mason*
Production/Composition: *Real Media Solutions*

Copy Editor: *Dina Forbes, WordPlayers*
Illustrator: *Larry Schwinger*
Cover Designer: *Bill Brammer Design*
Printer: *Webcom*

Printed in Canada.
2 3 4 5 6 7 8 9 10   06 05 04 03 02

For more information contact Heinle, 25 Thomson Place, Boston, Massachusetts 02210 USA, or you can visit our Internet site at http://www.heinle.com

For permission to use material from this text or product, contact us:
Tel   1-800-730-2214
Fax   1-800-730-2215
Web http://www.thomsonrights.com

Library of Congress Control Number:
2001093101
ISBN: 0-03-033987-1

Contents

Introduction

Steps to Academic Reading 1, Steps and Plateaus is a basic reading text for new readers of English. Written for the young adult and adult ESL/EFL student, this book features general vocabulary, the words that new learners of English already know or need and want to know. Through theme-based units (called Steps) and nonspecialized subject matter, adult students find familiar content an aid to learning to read in English. Summary recycling of the themes and vocabulary occurs in the Plateaus.

Steps to Academic Reading 1, Steps and Plateaus is a series of relevant topics in readings with very low but gradually increasing readability levels. The highest-frequency words in English are used in simple but natural sentences, reinforcing their meaning. Vocabulary items outside of the basic list are defined in context and illustrated in the graphics. The main objective of this text is to help students develop the language and thinking skills that they need to become successful, proficient readers of English. *Steps to Academic Reading 1, Steps and Plateaus,* therefore, focuses on the following aspects of reading:

- fostering the interaction between the reader and the text,
- getting the gist of a topic,
- drawing key concepts out of a reading,
- making connections between ideas,
- figuring out the meanings of words and the idiomatic usage from context,
- learning specialized reading strategies like reading for details or sequence,
- learning to tolerate ambiguity and use minimal clues for understanding.

Above all, reading *Steps to Academic Reading 1, Steps and Plateaus* is learning to read words in meaning groups to improve reading speed and efficiency. In this reading text, students begin with just a few hundred words and expand to a vocabulary of 1500 words.

The Organization of the Book

The outline of *Steps to Academic Reading 1, Steps and Plateaus* is simple: there are fifteen progressive Steps, or short thematic units, and three Plateaus, larger thematic units with greater variety in readings, activity types, and vocabulary development materials. The Plateaus are expansions of the themes of the Steps, thus providing opportunities for respiraling and extending the concepts and the vocabulary. Each set of five Steps is followed by a Plateau.

Special Features for the Beginning Reader

To promote successful reading experiences for the reader who is just beginning to read in English, a teacher must select easy material. However, that material must be simple in sentence structure, particularly tenses and embedded structures. Because students benefit from practicing with familiar forms before new forms are introduced, the grammatical forms in the first part of *Steps to Academic Reading 1, Steps and Plateaus* have generally been limited to simple present tense statements and questions, simple past tense statements and questions, and future meaning with *will*. As the text progresses, somewhat more complex forms are introduced. The purpose is to help students develop critical reading skills by providing plenty of practice with simple and familiar forms. That is why the following characteristics, which facilitate processing of the printed word and lower the level of readability (accessibility), form the basis of the presentation.

- Sentence length has been limited so that the concept load of each sentence is manageable by the beginning reader. If a student can process a sentence of five to eight words in ten seconds, then he or she is unlikely to need to write down the meanings of the words. For this reason, sentences are very short in the first Steps. These sentences are not necessarily authentic text, but they are understandable chunks of language that will give new readers a sense of success because they will be able to read and understand them. As learners succeed in reading and understanding, their confidence and enjoyment increase.

- Simple transition words such as *and, but,* and *so* are occasionally used to begin sentences and to include a feeling of continuity. Similarly, there are few embedded structures in the first set of Steps, and those that are there are heavily supported by the context. As students progress through the text, they are able to read longer sentences and able to understand combined ideas; therefore, because clauses and *if/then* constructions are added to their repertoire, not overtly as elements of grammar, but inductively as ways to combine two ideas.

- Each reading is followed by a set of questions. If the answer to a question is stated within the reading, the student might be asked to write the answer. However, because many answers are actually inferences, and because students might not have the active vocabulary with which to express their ideas, a multiple-choice format is used for the reader to read and to select from. Thus the students are dealing with ideas that may be beyond their active ability to express, while their passive fluency and ultimately their active language ability are being increased.

Suggested Procedures for Use of *Steps to Academic Reading 1, Steps and Plateaus*

The following techniques and strategies work well with this text:

▶ Prereading

Create an anticipatory set of words and phrases related to the topic. As an introduction to a Step or Plateau, have your students focus on the titles and the illustrations of the unit. Many of the target vocabulary items and the concepts are presented there. Brainstorm as a class. With the students' input, write words and phrases on the board. As you write, you might want to group the words and phrases that are related. You can point to parts of an illustration and ask students what they see or read a title and ask what the title might mean. Such an open class brainstorming session is a particularly productive way of eliciting the predictable and related concepts. Students will listen to what their classmates have to say and volunteer ideas of their own, thus increasing the total background knowledge of each student. In this way, the semantic mapping that occurs among related concepts begins to form internally.

► Reading

At first, you might consider reading the text articles aloud to your students. Ask your students to read along with you or to examine the illustrations. Pause to indicate illustrations of key concepts as you go through the reading for the first time. Read slowly but with a natural intonation. Pause after each sentence, allowing students time to process the complete sentence units. If it seems appropriate, read the story aloud a second and third time, and encourage the students to read it aloud quietly as you read. In any one class there are likely to be students who have greater and lesser degrees of proficiency in reading. Those who already understand the keys to reading will not benefit as much from the repeated reading as those who are developing readers. Students with greater proficiency might be asked to copy the text and to combine sentences, making the text more complex and helping them learn more about sentence structure.

Students whose language ability is being stretched by the reading will also be gaining a useful skill. They will begin to recognize that they do not need to understand the meaning of every word and every sentence to gain information from the reading. This tolerance for ambiguity is an essential skill for every language learner. Although it might occasionally be useful to allow the use of bilingual dictionary, encourage judicious and not continual use of the tool so that students feel more at ease with the readings but not dependent on their dictionaries.

► Activity Types

Within each **Step** and **Plateau**, you will find a variety of exercise types, though not all units have the same format. There is enough variety to prevent boredom. The teacher can select different kinds of exercises for individual or group work. Some exercises are most effectively done as a class. Some work well as assigned homework. In each **Step** and **Plateau** there are ideas for individuals to relate their lives to the theme.

≈| Let's Learn from the Reading!

The main points of the reading are the focus in these questions: important details, meanings of new words, main idea, sequences, and simple inferences. Because students do not always have the active vocabulary and oral fluency needed to express what they have understood, the language is sometimes provided for them, in multiple-choice questions.

Let's Practice!

This section is usually a number of different exercises, designed to give plenty of opportunity for practice in using new words, understanding details, categorizing, and applying principles that have been learned or implied in the reading.

Let's Talk!

Through these sections, students can relate the ideas in the reading to their own lives. These questions can be used to stimulate in-class discussions and to create contexts for the new vocabulary to be used in conversation. Some of the questions are anticipatory of ideas that will soon become a part of the classwork.

Let's Write!

Reading and writing are related skills. The activities in these sections integrate writing into the development of reading skills. In general, the writing activities are guided tasks that recycle the main concepts. The topics for students to write on are clearly defined. The activities are designed to foster successful writing experiences by limiting the amount of material that the students have to create and compose themselves. At the same time, students are guided into creating personal responses to what they have read.

Let's Think!

The emphasis in these exercises is on developing critical thinking skills.

Let's Find Out About You!

These questions invite students to explore their emotional responses to aspects of the theme.

Extension Activities

In some **Steps** and **Plateaus** there are extra readings, games, and charts to read and understand. These activities typically provide extra practice with the words and ideas so as to help students become more comfortable with the learning. Some of these activities are appropriate for homework.

Steps and Plateaus makes relevant information about everyday life accessible to the new reader of English. The simple beginning-level readings and the skill-building and integrating activities help students build the foundation for success in reading in English.

Acknowledgments

Special thanks to Barbara L. Sosna, my co-author in creating the first readings for raw beginners. And thanks to the in-home support team of one, my husband John.

I would also like to thank Phyllis Dobbins, Matt Drapeau, Sherrise Roehr, Charlotte Sturdy, and Angela Urquhart of Heinle; Robert Bovasso, Elizabeth Geary, and Conni Wynn-Smith of Real Media Solutions; and Jacqueline Flamm and Dina Forbes of WordPlayers.

Step 1

Before You Read

1. Why are names important?
2. How many names do most people have? What are they?
3. What do we name?

The Day Family

1　　Hello! My name is John Day. This is my wife. Her name is Margaret. We are married. So we are Mr. and Mrs. Day. Before our marriage, she was Margaret Long. Now she uses my last name. Day is our family name. We are

5　husband and wife.

　　My whole name is John Henry Day. John is my first name. Henry is my middle name. Middle names come between first and last names. Day is my last name. Margaret has a beautiful middle name. It is Elizabeth.

10　　People usually have two names. Some have three. We have three names.

　　We have two children. Our little boy is Johnny. Our son and I have the same name. He is John Henry Day, Junior. I am John Henry Day, Senior. Our little girl is a

15　baby. She is very small. Her name is Alison. She has a middle name. It is Long. She has part of her mother's name. Long is Margaret's maiden name.

　　We have names from our families. Margaret's mother is Alice Long. My father is Henry Day.

20　　We live in a small city. Its name is Niagara. It is in Wisconsin. We live on River Street. We have a big river in Niagara. It is the Menominee River. The river is between Michigan and Wisconsin. They are two states.

　　Do we need names? Of course! We all have names.

25　Cities have names. Streets have names. Big buildings have names. We even give names to animals. My family has a dog. His name is Max. He is a nice dog.

Names are interesting. They are useful. We need
names for people and places. With names, we can talk
30   about people. We can ask for things. We can talk about
places, too. Names are important. We need them. We use
them every day.

Let's Learn from the Reading!

Here are some questions for you. They are about the reading. Do you
understand the reading? Use the questions to understand.

1. How many names do people usually have?

   _____

2. How many names does each person in the Day family have?

   _____

3. What is Mrs. Day's first name?

   _____

4. What is the main idea of the reading?
   a. Buildings, people, and places have names.
   b. People have a lot of names.
   c. We need names to talk about things.
   d. A little boy has his father's name.

5. Alison is...
   a. ten years old.   c. six years old.
   b. three months old.   d. twelve years old.

6. Who is Margaret Elizabeth Long now?

   _____

7. How many children do the Days have?

   _____

8. What is Mr. Day's middle name?

   _____

9. What does *Senior* after a name mean?

    a. A boy and his mother have one name.

    b. A son has his father's name.

    c. *Junior* means "important."

    d. Junior is a baby name.

10. Whose maiden name is Long?

    _____

11. What is Alison's middle name?

    _____

12. What is Alison's whole name?

    _____

13. Who is Max?

    _____

14. Read these names: Alice, Elizabeth, Margaret, Alison. These names are all...

    a. last names.　　　　　　c. women's names.

    b. boys' names.　　　　　　d. names for men.

Let's Practice!

Here is some more practice for you. These are exercises. You can practice your English with these exercises.

A. *True* or *False*?

Does the information follow the facts of the reading? Write *true* in the blanks for those sentences. Some sentences do NOT follow the information in the reading. Write *false* in the blanks for those sentences.

1. __true__　Cities have names.

2. _____　A husband's last name is usually the family name.

3. _____　We use names to talk about people.

4. _____　Some streets do not have names.

5. _____ Mr. Day is married.

6. _____ The Days have a daughter and a son.

7. _____ Mrs. Day has a wife.

8. _____ A woman's maiden name is a last name.

9. _____ Michigan is a city.

10. _____ There is a river between Michigan and Wisconsin.

B. Find the Different Word

One word in each group is different. Can you find it? Put a circle around it.

1.	man	(people)	woman	child
2.	talk	speak	name	mean
3.	first	important	middle	last
4.	baby	boy	family	child
5.	about	to	with	his
6.	you	we	the	she
7.	two	first	three	one
8.	son	father	mother	husband
9.	Margaret	Johnny	John	Henry
10.	Alison	Margaret	Henry	Elizabeth
11.	Day	Margaret	John	Alison
12.	small	big	very	little

C. Find Things with Names

Draw a circle around all the things with names.

(family)	person	house	dog	book	state
mother	father	pencil	city	friend	river
husband	school	paper	son	street	baby
teacher	people	girl	boy	wife	letter
daughter	child	idea	cat		

D. Find the Same Meaning

Draw a line between the two words or phrases with similar meanings.

1. Junior

2. a baby

3. a maiden name

4. a whole name

5. a middle name

6. a son

7. a girl child

8. a married man

a. a daughter

b. a name between the first and last names

c. A boy and his father have the same name.

d. first, middle, and last names

e. a very small child

f. a boy child

g. a woman's last name before marriage

h. a husband

E.   Names and Addresses

1. A letter comes to you in the mail. It is in an envelope. There are many names on the envelope.

   a. Is your name on the envelope? _____

   b. Are there other names on the envelope? _____

   c. What are the names on your envelope? _____

2. Look at the names on this envelope.

Mr. John H. Day, Sr.
1600 River St.
Niagara, Wisconsin 54151
USA

        Ms. Josie J. Faust
        301-1542 West 10th
        Vancouver, British Columbia
        V6H 1N9 CANADA

a. Who sent the letter? _____

b. What word does *Sr.* at the end of his name mean? _____

c. What street does he live on? _____

d. What city does he live in? _____

e. What country does he live in? _____

f. Niagara is in the state of _____

g. Who is the letter for? _____

h. Is it for a man or a woman? _____

i. Vancouver is in _____

j. The middle names of the people are not on the envelope. Only the first letters of the middle names are there. What letters do their middle names begin with?

_____

3. Addresses have postal codes. For example, the U.S. Post Office uses ZIP codes. ZIP codes are postal codes. The ZIP code for Niagara, Wisconsin, is 54151. Niagara is very small. It has only one number. The number helps the post office.

   a. A big city has many postal codes. Vancouver is a big city. What is one postal code for Vancouver? _____

   b. Does your address have a postal code? _____

      If so, what is it? _____

Let's Talk!

A. Names Around the World

In some countries, names are different. They are not like Margaret Day's name. For example, Wu Ming-Ming is a Chinese woman. Wu is her family name. In English, she is Miss Wu or Ms. Wu.

Wang Shinian is a Chinese man. He is Mr. _____ .

B. Names in Your Class

Talk with people in your classroom. Learn about them. Here are some questions to ask.

1. What is your first name? Is it your family name?
2. What is your whole name?
3. What do you use with your name—Mr., Mrs., Miss, or Ms.?

Let's Write!

A letter comes for John Day. It is from Henry J. Childs. The Days live at 1600 River Street in Niagara, Wisconsin. Their ZIP code is 54151. Read the letter.

---

890 First St.

Ironwood, Michigan 48922

September 3

Dear Mr. Day,

    Let me introduce myself. I am Henry James Childs. My father is James John Childs. His father was George Matthew Childs. He and my grandmother were married in 1942 in Ohio.

    My grandmother's name was Martha Maria. Her maiden name was Day. Her mother's and father's names were Angela and Henry.

    Your family name is like mine, Day. Are you and I from the same family? Please write me a letter.

        Sincerely,

        Henry James Childs

        Henry James Childs

Write a letter to Mr. Childs from Mr. Day. John Day's grandfather was Robert H. Day. He had a sister. Her name was Martha.

Dear _____ ,

_____

_____

_____

_____

_____

_____

_____

_____

_____

Yours sincerely,

_____

Write the envelope. Write John Day's address on the first lines.
Write Henry Childs's address on the other lines.

_____

_____

_____

        _____

        _____

        _____

Let's Find Out About You!

Fill in the blanks. Introduce yourself to other people in the class.

- Where do you live?
- What is your address?

- What things do you enjoy?
- Tell about your family.

About Me

Hello, I am glad to meet you! My name is

_____ . I live in

_____ . My address is
(city or country)

_____

_____ .

I am happy. I like sports and music, too.

And I like to read in _____ . I

enjoy it very much.

This is my family. I have a nice mother

and _____ . I _____
(have/don't have)

_____   _____
(brother/brothers)   (and/or)
_____ . I love my family.
(sister/sisters)

I am a student like you. It is nice to meet

you.

Good-bye!

Step 2

Before You Read

1. In a city, where are there lots of books in one place?
2. How can you find some books at the library?
3. Why are libraries usually quiet?

Come to the Library

1　　Come to the library. Please come in. Are you a student? This is a good place to study. Please, close the door softly. Everyone is quiet here. Students study in quiet places.

　　There are many books here. There are many different
5　kinds. You can use them for your classes. There are books about other countries, like Japan and Mexico. You can find history books, too. Take one. Read about the old days. Or read a literature book. Read stories. Stories are one kind of literature.

10　　The library is a quiet place. So it is a good place to study. Many students come here. They use the computers. They read school books of all kinds. For example, they read philosophy books. They read the big art books, too. The students study their lessons. They find answers to
15　questions in books. There is a big dictionary, too. It is on a special little table. It's in the corner. There is information at the library for students' papers.

　　There are librarians here. Librarians help students. They know all about books. They can find information fast. They
20　help students with their work.

　　One librarian is Bill Church. Bill is a quiet man. But you can talk to him. You can even call him on the telephone. You can ask him questions. He will help you. He finds answers to questions. He uses the computers in the library.
25　He knows answers to many questions. He can find books and information fast.

There are many things to do. You can read for fun. You can look at pictures. You can play on the computers. But don't talk loud! Libraries are quiet places for people to
30   read. A person must not talk loud in a library. A person must whisper. Go to the library, and enjoy it. But please, be quiet for other people.

 Let's Learn from the Reading!

Here are some questions for you. They are about the reading. Do you understand the reading?

1. Students come to the library...
   a. to talk loud.   c. to read for fun.
   b. to study and find answers.   d. to talk about librarians.

2. What is a library? It is...
   a. a big dictionary.   c. an art book.
   b. a place to talk.   d. a place for books.

3. What is the main idea of "Come to the Library"?
   a. There are art books in a library.
   b. A library is a quiet place to read.
   c. A librarian works in a library.
   d. Libraries have big dictionaries.

4. Why are people quiet in a library?
   a. Mr. Church is a quiet man.
   b. People read and study in a library.
   c. Don't talk in libraries.
   d. A librarian is in the library.

5. Which sentence is in "Come to the Library"? Find the sentence in the reading and underline it.

   a. It is on a special little table.

   b. Students study here at night.

   c. He is a big man.

   d. Please don't be quiet.

6. What is the librarian's name in the reading? _____

7. Bill Church is a _____ man. He doesn't talk much.

8. What does *literature* mean?

   a. don't talk much   c. stories

   b. be quiet   d. a big book

9. What kinds of books are in the library? (Circle all the right answers.)

   a. There are big books.   d. There are philosophy books.

   b. There are history books.   e. There are literature books.

   c. There are art books.   f. There are small books.

10. *To talk in a quiet voice* means…

    a. to study.   c. to be quiet.

    b. to whisper.   d. to read.

Let's Practice!

A. *True* or *False*?

Write *true* or *false* in each blank.

1. _____ People talk in a library. They don't whisper.

2. _____ Librarians are big philosophy books.

3. _____ Art books are usually large.

4. _____ Japan is one country, and Mexico is one other country.

5. _____ Students study in quiet places.

6. _____ Librarians do not use computers in their work.

7. _____ A librarian answers many questions.

8. _____ You can call the library on the telephone for answers to questions.

9. _____ *To whisper* means "to talk softly."

10. _____ All librarians must know how to find answers to many questions.

B. Find the Different Word

One word in each group is different. Can you find it? Put a circle around it. How are the other words like one another?

1.	talk	speak	whisper	quiet	
2.	art	history	philosophy	librarian	
3.	tables	students	librarians	people	
4.	it	of	about	for	to
5.	big	fun	softly	good	
6.	art	read	study	work	
7.	stories	literature	dictionaries		
8.	stories	answers	questions		
9.	all	fast	softly		
10.	ask	help	enjoy	kind	call

C. Things in a Library

There are many things in a library. Of course, there are many books. Libraries have different kinds of books. You can find other useful things there too. For example, libraries have pictures and maps. They have magazines and catalogs. There are even telephone books for other cities in some libraries. Many libraries have special programs for children. They have toys and children's books. Some libraries have special programs for students. Many have night programs so people can learn new things.

Here is a list of items. You can find some of these things in libraries. Draw a circle around things in libraries. Then talk about your answers with other people in your class.

classroom	dictionaries	maps
tables	post office	literature books
computers	chairs	quiet places
librarians	newspapers	telephone books
cats	history books	toys
books about art		

Can you think of other things? List them here:

_____

D. Find the Same Meaning

Draw a line between the two words or phrases with similar meanings.

1. a dictionary	a. don't speak
2. enjoy	b. one more
3. talk	c. whisper
4. history	d. read to learn
5. other	e. a book of words
6. a question	f. part of literature
7. quiet	g. like to do
8. talk quietly	h. information about the old days
9. study	i. Do you know?
10. story	j. speak

E. Find the Word

Fill in the blanks.

1. Ask someone a question. Then someone can _____ it.

2. Write a book. Then someone can _____ it.

3. Go to a computer. You can _____ with it.

4. Look in a dictionary. You can find many _____ in it.

5. Open an art book. You will find _____ in it.

6. Talk in the library. Someone will say, "Please be _____ !"

7. Go to a quiet library. You can _____ there.

8. Call the library with a question. A _____ will find the answer for you.

Let's Talk!

Talk with people in your classroom. Learn about them. Here are some questions.

1. What kinds of books do you read?

2. Is there a library near your house?
   What can you do there?
   Can you read magazines there?
   Does the library near your house have special programs for children?
   Are there also special programs for students there?

3. What do you enjoy at the library?

Let's Work on Numbers!

Let's learn some numbers:

1 = one	6 = six	11 = eleven	16 = sixteen
2 = two	7 = seven	12 = twelve	17 = seventeen
3 = three	8 = eight	13 = thirteen	18 = eighteen
4 = four	9 = nine	14 = fourteen	19 = nineteen
5 = five	10 = ten	15 = fifteen	20 = twenty

Let's practice with numbers. Complete these sentences. Fill in the blanks.

I have many books from the _____ . My

brother and sister do too! I have _____ (5) books.

My brother has _____ (12) books—all about

computers. My sister has only _____ (3). We

have _____ (20) books from the library. Here is

a letter from the librarian. "Please bring the _____

back to the library." Mother will help us. She has some books

from the library too— _____ (10 or 11). We will

go to the library in the car.

Let's Write!

Here is some information about the Niagara Public Library. You can find these things there:

- magazines of all kinds
- ten small desks
- a large dictionary
- five long tables
- maps and pictures
- four librarians
- a lot of chairs of different kinds
- twenty computers on little tables
- a special table for a big dictionary
- a room for children's books and toys
- 150,000 (one hundred fifty thousand) books

Now write about the Niagara Public Library. You can use sentences like these:

The Niagara Public Library has _____ .
There are _____ .
There is _____ .
It has _____ .
People can _____ .

The Public Library in Niagara

_____

_____

_____

_____

_____

_____

_____

_____

_____

_____

_____

_____

_____

Let's Find Out About You!

1. Think about your life, and make up a title for your story:

   _____

2. What country is special for you? _____

3. How can you find out about your country in the library?

   _____

   _____

   _____

   _____

   _____

   _____

   _____

Step 3

Before You Read

1. There are many things to read. Think of something fun and easy to read. What is it?

2. Why do people like magazines?

Let's Read Magazines

1   Do you like magazines? Most people do. Magazines have useful articles in them. They are fun to read. They have a lot of important information. The stories are interesting. And they are colorful. Most people get some magazines in 5 the mail. They buy magazines to read too. People read millions of magazines every month. They find out about new things.

There are many kinds of magazines. Some are news magazines. They give the news of the world. They tell 10 about important people and facts. News magazines are like newspapers. One big news magazine is *Time. Newsweek* is another. Do you read them? Do you know about them?

There are magazines for professional people. They are "journals." Journals have new ideas. Doctors, for example, 15 are professional people. And doctors have special magazines. For example, their journals have information about hospitals. There is information about new medicines. Doctors learn from their journals.

Farmers are professionals too. There are special maga- 20 zines for farmers. Farmers' journals give them new ideas for their farms. Farmers learn how to farm better from journals.

You can find other special magazines. For example, some clubs have their own magazines. There are also sports magazines. These magazines are popular. Many people 25 enjoy tennis. So they like to buy tennis magazines. Many people like golf. Golf magazines are also popular. Popular sports "sell" magazines. (People want to buy them!)

      Some magazines are for children. These magazines have interesting stories. Young people enjoy them. There
30   are also bright pictures in children's magazines. The words are easy too. Many people want to buy these magazines. They get them for their children. Why? It's simple. They want their children to read. Children can read them easily. They want to read them. They enjoy them. And they enjoy
35   reading.

      There are magazines just for men. They have articles about sports. Other articles are about ideas that are interesting for men. There are magazines only for women. These magazines have articles about careers. They have
40   articles about places to visit, too. They also have ideas for homes. They have pictures of things to make. Everyone likes magazines. They are fun to read. There are thousands of magazines. There are magazines for everyone.

≈| Let's Learn from the Reading!

Here are some questions for you. They are about the reading. Do you understand the reading? Can you answer these questions? The questions can help you to understand about magazines.

1. What are news magazines about? _____

   _____

2. Two popular sports are _____ and _____ .

3. What is the main idea of "Let's Read Magazines"?
   a. Professional people get magazines.
   b. Farmers read journals about farms.
   c. Children's magazines have beautiful pictures.
   d. Magazines are popular with most people.

4. Why do children's magazines have pictures?

    a. Children can't read.

    b. Children like bright pictures.

    c. Doctors read magazines for children.

    d. All magazines are for children.

5. Which sentence is in "Let's Read Magazines"? Find the sentence in the reading and underline it.

    a. There are important people in the world.

    b. Magazines tell about hospitals and medicines.

    c. There are special magazines for farmers.

    d. Many magazines are about tennis and golf.

6. Which magazines have articles? (Circle all the right answers.)

    a. magazines for everyone

    b. farmers' journals

    c. news magazines

    d. men's and women's magazines

    e. magazines for children

    f. professional journals

    g. journals for doctors

7. News magazines are like _____ .

8. "Magazines are popular." What does this mean?

    a. Many people like them and buy them.

    b. Farmers read magazines.

    c. Stories in magazines are interesting.

    d. They have bright pictures.

9. There are special magazines for _____ people— for example, doctors and farmers.

10. The words in children's magazines are _____ .

11. What does this sentence mean? "Popular sports sell magazines."

    a. People go to play sports and buy magazines there.

    b. People play sports to buy magazines.

    c. People like to read about sports.

    d. People can play and read at the same time.

12. Which of these words is the name of a career? (Circle all the right answers.)

    a. doctor   d. farmer

    b. journal   e. man

    c. librarian

 Let's Read More!

Professional Journals

1   Groups of professional people have special magazines. Professional people like doctors and teachers need special information. A magazine for a group of professionals has another name. It is a *journal*.

5   Journals have information for special groups. Professionals learn from the articles in journals. For example, doctors get the latest information on medicines. Teachers get information about new books. They also get new ideas for their classes. Journals are very important for
10   professional people. Doctors, teachers, farmers, lawyers, dentists, and pharmacists read their professional journals. Professionals cannot go to school every year, but they need to learn about new things. So they keep up with their professions by reading articles in journals.

Let's Learn from the Reading!

Answer these questions with information from the reading.

1. What is a journal? _____

   _____

2. Who are some professional people? _____

   _____

3. Why is it important for professionals to read their journals?

   _____

Let's Practice!

A. *True* or *False?*

Write *true* or *false* in each blank.

1. _____ Magazines are fun to read.

2. _____ Sports magazines are popular.

3. _____ Many women read sports magazines.

4. _____ Young children read sports magazines.

5. _____ Children's magazines have interesting pictures.

6. _____ Many people's magazines come in the mail.

7. _____ Farmers don't have farming journals.

8. _____ Children's magazines have easy words.

9. _____ People can buy magazines.

10. _____ Tennis is a sport.

11. _____ Philosophy books are popular with children.

12. _____ There are magazines for people to read and enjoy at a library.

B. Find the Different Word

One word is different. Can you find it? Put a circle around it. How are the other words like one another? Talk with another person in the class about your ideas.

1.	newspaper	magazine	idea	book	
2.	pharmacist	children	doctor	farmer	
3.	important	popular	farm	big	
4.	tennis	home	golf		
5.	about	many	a lot	all	
6.	popular	enjoy	want	like	
7.	want	give	like	news	read
8.	about	have	for	at	
9.	medicine	hospital	world	doctor	
10.	woman	doctor	child	man	
11.	interesting	simple	easy		
12.	colorful	special	bright		
13.	important	many	most	some	
14.	thousands	millions	clubs		

 ## Let's Write!

Read this list. It is a list of ideas for magazine articles. Which articles do you want to read?

stories about professional women	help for mothers
pictures of new clothes	ideas for farms
maps of many countries	articles about food
bright pictures for children	news stories
information about new medicines	farm information
articles about careers	ideas for family fun
new ideas for homes	English lessons
information about new books	new ideas for farms
information about hospitals	hospital facts

stories for young people	articles about sports
ideas for things to make	career information
information about children	news stories
pictures of new clothes	stories for children
information about books	history articles

Make two lists, *Articles I Want to Read* and *Articles I Don't Want to Read*. Write sentences like these:

I want to read about <u>ideas for farms</u>. I like <u>to farm</u>.

I don't want to read about <u>ideas for farms</u>. I don't like <u>to farm</u>.

Write the sentences here:

Articles I Want to Read

_____

_____

_____

Articles I Don't Want to Read

_____

_____

_____

Find Other Words with These Meanings

Look in the two readings. Find a word or phrase with a similar meaning.

1. story = _____

2. journal = _____

3. very young people = _____

4. news = _____

5. golf and tennis = _____

6. doctors, farmers, teachers = _____

7. *Time* and *Newsweek* = _____

8. men, women, and children = _____

9. simple = _____

10. buy = _____

Think About Professional People

Doctors and teachers are professional people. Can you name other kinds of professional people?

Make a list of professional people here:

_____   _____

_____   _____

_____   _____

Talk with another person in your class. Do you have the same professions in your lists?

Let's Work with Numbers!

Learn some more numbers:

20 = twenty	60 = sixty	100 = one hundred
30 = thirty	70 = seventy	1000 = one thousand
40 = forty	80 = eighty	1,000,000 = one million
50 = fifty	90 = ninety	

Learn these three things:

+ is "plus."   = is "equals."   – is "minus."

Write the numbers in words. Read them to another person.

1. 20 + 30 = __fifty__

__Twenty__ __plus__ __thirty__ equals __fifty__ .

2. 30 + 40 = _____

   _____ _____ _____ equals _____ .

3. 90 − 20 = _____

   _____ _____ _____ equals _____ .

4. 80 − 60 = _____

   _____ _____ _____ equals _____ .

5. 60 + 40 = _____

   _____ _____ _____ equals _____ .

6. 50 + 30 = _____

   _____ _____ _____ equals _____ .

7. 60 − 20 = _____

   _____ _____ _____ equals _____ .

8. 20 + 60 = _____

   _____ _____ _____ equals _____ .

9. 30 + 70 = _____

   _____ _____ _____ equals _____ .

10. 80 − 60 = _____

   _____ _____ _____ equals _____ .

 Let's Find Out About You!

1. What profession do you want for yourself?
2. How many months old are you? How can you find out?
   (12 months = 1 year)

Step 4

Before you Read

1. How do schools change?
2. How are schools today different from schools 200 years ago?
3. What new things make learning easier?

Schools Then and Now

1   Today's schools are very good places to learn. They have things to help teachers and students. For example, students have books. They use them at school. They can even take them home. There are big blackboards at school.
5   Teachers write on them. The students have pencils. They have lots of paper. Students today even have computers. Today students really have everything to make learning easy.

    Two hundred years ago, schools were different. Many
10   schools didn't have anything then. There were not many books, for example. Books were really expensive. They cost a lot of money, so many students did not have books. Students had some paper. But not much. And it wasn't cheap! And no one had a pencil. There were no pencils
15   then. Students wrote with ink. They used bird feathers (quills) to make pens.

    Some schools had maps and dictionaries. They also had pictures of famous people in the classrooms.

    Students and teachers had desks and tables. But their
20   classrooms didn't have big blackboards. Students used slates. These were small blackboards. Each student had one. Slates were cheap. Students wrote lessons on them. It was necessary for them to use their slates. They used them many times. After all, paper was not cheap. Students
25   sat at their desks all day. They wrote notes on their slates. The teacher watched them. The teacher helped them. The teacher talked to the students. That's how teachers gave lessons. The students just listened—most of the time.

30 Two hundred years ago, schools did not even have clocks. Homes didn't have clocks either. When did the students go to school? In the morning, the teacher rang the school bell. Students listened for it. They stayed home until the bell rang. Then they left home. They stayed at

35 school all day. They studied hard. Students didn't leave school until late in the afternoon. They studied at home in the evening.

The school year was different too. Children had school only in the winter. It was necessary for them to work at

40 other times. That's why the school day was long.

Today's schools are different in many ways. The school year is about nine months long. The school day is short. In schools today, students work on computers. They often watch videos. They talk about ideas and learn from one

45 another too. Schools are not the same now.

Let's Learn from the Reading!

Here are some questions for you. They are about the reading. Do you understand the reading? Can you answer these questions?

1. What do students read in schools or at home?

   _____

2. What does *expensive* mean?

   _____

3. What does *cheap* mean?

   _____

4. What is "Schools Then and Now" about?

    a. Schools are expensive for teachers.

    b. Schools have maps and pictures and dictionaries.

    c. All children like school.

    d. Schools were different 200 years ago.

5. Two hundred years ago, students did not write on paper. Why not?

    a. They liked their slates and liked to use them.

    b. The teacher watched them.

    c. No one had a pencil to write with.

    d. Paper was too expensive for students to use.

6. Students didn't have pencils. They wrote with _____ and ink.

7. Which sentence is in "Schools Then and Now"? Find the sentence in the reading and underline it.

    a. They wrote notes on their slates.

    b. The teacher watched the students.

    c. Schools didn't have many books 200 years ago.

    d. The students listened for the school bell.

8. What time of day did the students go to school? _____

9. When did the students go home? _____

10. What is a feather? What does it come from?

    a. A feather is like a bell.

    b. Feathers come from clocks.

    c. A feather comes from a bird.

    d. A feather comes from a desk.

11. A slate is like a small _____ .

12. How is a slate like a small blackboard?

    a. A slate is big.

    b. Students and teachers like slates.

    c. People write with ink on slates.

    d. People can write on slates.

13. A slate is different from a blackboard. How?
    a. A blackboard is big, and a slate is small.
    b. Slates are black and expensive.
    c. Blackboards are cheap to buy.
    d. Teachers write on blackboards.

14. Two hundred years ago, the school year was _____ ,
    and the school day was _____ .

15. Today's schools have _____ and _____
    to help students learn.

Let's Practice!

A. *True* or *False*?

Write *true* or *false* in each blank.

1. _____ Today's students have videos, so they do not need books.

2. _____ Paper is too expensive for students to use today.

3. _____ Pencils are for writing on slates.

4. _____ Today's schools do not have maps and dictionaries.

5. _____ Students today write on slates.

6. _____ Quills are popular with students today.

7. _____ Teachers don't use school bells today.

8. _____ Two hundred years ago, the school year was short, and
   the school day was long.

B. Find the Different Word

One word in each group is different from the other words. Find it. Put a circle around it. How is it different from the other words? How are the other words like one another?

1.	dictionaries	books	teachers	
2.	desk	table	picture	
3.	afternoon	morning	evening	today
4.	expensive	small	big	
5.	student	teacher	clock	
6.	paper	pen	pencil	
7.	different	with	on	at
8.	school	listen	watch	give
9.	have	had	has	is
10.	classroom	hundred	school	
11.	dictionary	picture	map	
12.	expensive	cost	cheap	

C. Find Other Words with These Meanings

Find a word or phrase with a similar meaning.

1. table = _____

2. not expensive = _____

3. not like = _____

4. not small = _____

5. not to stay = _____

6. bird-feather pen = _____

D. Find the Word

Fill in the blanks.

1. Two _____ years ago, there was not much in a classroom.

2. The students did not have many _____ to read.

3. They did not have money to buy _____ .

4. Students did not have much _____ to write on.

5. They wrote with _____ feathers and ink.

6. There were no _____ at home or at school.

7. In the morning, students listened for the school _____ .

8. They stayed at school all _____ .

9. The students left school late in the _____ .

10. Students studied at home in the _____ .

11. Two hundred years ago, students didn't have _____ to watch and learn from.

12. There were no _____ to help them learn to write either.

Let's Talk!

Talk with another person in your class. Do you have the same ideas?

1. Do you like to read books? How many books do you have?

2. Do you like to write on a blackboard? Why or why not?

3. What are some differences between schools today and schools 200 years ago?

Let's Read More!

Here is one month on a calendar. Every calendar tells the names of the months. It gives the days of the week, too. There are twelve months in a year. Each month has about thirty days. Some months have 31 numbers for the days of the week. Let's practice these numbers, too.

May						
Sunday	**Monday**	**Tuesday**	**Wednesday**	**Thursday**	**Friday**	**Saturday**
			1	2	3	4
5	6	7	8	9	10	11
12	13	14	15	16	17	18
19	20	21	22	23	24	25
26	27	28	29	30	31	

Numbers and the Calendar

One = 1.   The **first** month of the year is JANUARY.
                  It has 31 days.

Two = 2.   The **second** month of the year is FEBRUARY.
                  It is a short month. It has 28 or 29 days.
                  Every four years, February has one more day.

Three = 3.   The **third** month of the year is MARCH.
                  It has 31 days.

Four = 4.   The **fourth** month of the year is APRIL.
                  It has 30 days.

Five = 5.   The **fifth** month of the year is MAY.
                  It has 31 days.

Six = 6.   The **sixth** month of the year is JUNE.
                  It has 30 days.

Seven = 7.   The **seventh** month of the year is JULY.
                  It has 31 days.

Eight = 8.   The **eighth** month of the year is AUGUST.
                  It has 31 days.

Nine = 9.   The **ninth** month of the year is SEPTEMBER.
                  It has 30 days.

Ten = 10.   The **tenth** month of the year is OCTOBER.
                  It has 31 days.

Eleven = 11.   The **eleventh** month of the year is NOVEMBER.
                  It has 30 days.

Twelve = 12.   The **twelfth** and last month of the year is DECEMBER.
                  It has 31 days.

Here is a question for you. Four months have only 30 days. Seven months have 31 days. How many months have 28 days? The answer is at the end of this Step.

Let's Read Even More!

1   Every week has seven days. In North America the first day of the week is Sunday. Monday is the second day of the week. It is the first day of the work week. Tuesday is the third day of the week. And the fourth day is Wednesday. 5 Thursday is the fifth day of the week. Friday is the sixth day of the week. It is the last day of the work week. Saturday is the seventh day of the week. Saturday and Sunday are weekend days. The other days are weekdays. Calendars are not the same everywhere. For example, in 10 Japan Saturday is a work day. In Muslim countries, like Egypt and Saudi Arabia, Friday is a special day. No one works on Fridays there. Friday and Saturday are weekend days. In Israel, no one works on Saturday.

 Let's Talk!

Talk with another student in your classroom. Do you have the same ideas?

1. What is the "weekend" in your country?
2. What do you do on weekends?
3. How many days are in the work week?

Let's Practice!

A. The Weekdays
Fill in the blanks.

1. Every week has _____ days.

2. In North America, the _____ day of the week is Sunday.

3. Monday is the _____ day of the week. It is also the first day of the work week.

4. _____ is the third day of the week. And the fourth day is Wednesday.

5. _____ is the fifth day of the week.

6. Friday is the _____ day of the week.

7. It is the _____ day of the work week.

8. Saturday is the _____ day of the week.

9. _____ and _____ are weekend days in Canada, the U.S., and Mexico.

10. Monday, Tuesday, Wednesday, Thursday, and Friday are

    _____ days.

11. And Saturday and Sunday are the _____ .

12. There are about _____ weeks in a month.

B. The Months of the Year

Fill in the blanks with numbers and names of months.

1. There are _____ months in a year.

2. The first month is _____ .

3. The _____ month is February.

4. The _____ and _____ months are March and April.

5. The _____ month is May.

6. June is the _____ month.

7. July and _____ are the seventh and _____ months.

8. The _____ month is September.

9. Then it is _____ , the _____ month.

10. November is the _____ month.

11. The twelfth and _____ month of the year is _____ .

12. In which month were you born? _____

Let's Write!

A. *Now* or *Then*?

Here is a list of ideas for you to read. Some of these ideas are about school now *(now)*. Other ideas are about schools 200 years ago *(then)*. Write *Now* or *Then* in each blank in front of each item. Then write about *Schools Now* and *Schools Then* on your own paper. Use the ideas in this list.

1. _____ not much paper

2. _____ not many books

3. _____ lots of books

4. _____ no blackboards

5. _____ no slates

6. _____ lots of paper

7. _____ bird-feather quill pens and ink

8. _____ videos to watch and learn from

9. _____ computers in the classrooms

10. _____ a library with books

11. _____ big blackboards on the wall

12. _____ no clocks but a school bell

13. _____ pencils to write with

14. _____ books that students can take home

B. The Days of the Week

Copy these sentences. (Write them in your notebook or on paper.)
Fill in the blanks.

1. In North America the _____ day of the week is
   Sunday.

2. _____ is the second day of the week.

3. Tuesday is the _____ day of the week.

4. The fourth day of the week is _____ .

5. Thursday is the _____ day of the week.

6. The last day of the work week is _____ .

7. It is the _____ day of the week.

8. The _____ and last day of the week is Saturday.

9. There are _____ days in a weekend: Saturday and
   Sunday.

10. There are _____ days in the work week.

Let's Find Out About You!

1. What does your school have to help you learn?
2. How do you like to learn?

Answer: Every month has 28 days. (That is, all twelve months do. They all have 27 days, too.)

Step 5

Before You Read

1. Think of a world without calendars.
   What is it like?

2. Why were calendars important years ago?

Calendars

1　　What do you know about the calendar? Calendars are very old. And they are really interesting! There is important information on calendars. There are symbols on them. The symbols are numbers and pictures. The symbols give

5　meaning to the special days. There are facts about time and the world in the numbers on a calendar.

　　Many years ago, in Roman times, the people in Asia (China and India) had calendars. At that time, there were four important groups of people. These groups were the

10　farmers, the men of the church, the traders, and the king's family. They all needed to know about the seasons. They knew about spring, summer, fall, and winter. But they did not understand the reasons for the change of seasons.

　　How did calendars begin? Wise people studied the stars

15　and the moon. They made calendars to help people in business and farming. They began with the stars. The stars helped people remember important facts about the year. The stars tell the seasons. Farmers, for example, needed to know about the stars and how they changed. They

20　watched the stars and the changes in the stars. A group of stars comes with spring. Then farmers understood that it was time for planting. So they went to work in the fields.

25　　Understanding these changes was important for farmers. They needed to know about seasons; they needed to plant crops in their fields.

30   The moon was also important for farmers. Farmers looked for a night without a moon. They knew to plant some crops the next day. Then these plants grew well. Other crops, like flowers, grew well with or without the
35   moon.

Farmers marked the number of nights between full moons. They could see a pattern. There is a new moon every 29½ days. They called the time between two full moons a month. Twelve months made a year. However,
40   29½ times 12 equals 354 days (29.5 x 12 = 354)! And the year (the time for the Earth to go all the way around the sun) is 365¼ days. So every year there was a mistake of 11 days. The moon calendar was wrong.

Like farmers, the men of the church needed a calendar.
45   They wanted to know the days for holidays. A calendar helps people to remember important days. Of course, traders needed a calendar too, for business. The king needed a calendar for his business too.

Today the English-speaking world uses a different
50   calendar. There are 12 months. Seven months have 31 days. Four have 30 days. And February has 28 days for three years and 29 days for one year. So we have a calendar with 365 days three years out of four. The year with 366 days is Leap Year.

55   The calendar helps people remember important facts. For example, think about the year. There are fifty-two weeks in a year. There are four seasons in a year. There is also meaning in the colors on the calendar. Weekdays are black and holidays are red. Red is for special days. People
60   use calendars every day.

Let's Learn from the Reading!

Here are some questions for you. They are about the reading. Do you understand the reading? The questions can help you to understand it.

1. What has twelve months? _____

2. What has fifty-two weeks? _____

3. What are the seasons of the year? _____

   _____

4. What is the main idea of "Calendars"?

   a. A year has twelve months.

   b. Calendars have numbers and symbols.

   c. There were calendars in Asia before Europe.

   d. Calendars are important for all people today.

5. Why did farmers watch the stars?

   a. We see different stars in every season.

   b. Farmers do not read.

   c. The first calendars were about stars.

   d. Stars have meaning.

6. Which sentence is in "Calendars"? Find the sentence in the reading and underline it.

   a. Calendars and stars are interesting.

   b. So we have a calendar with 365 days three years out of four.

   c. Calendars have pictures, symbols, and numbers on them.

   d. Today's calendars look different from Chinese calendars.

7. On a calendar the weekdays are _____ . Red

   numbers are for Sundays and _____ .

8. People in business sell things. Another word for these people is…

   a. the king's family.

   b. spring, summer, fall, and winter.

   c. traders.

   d. churchmen.

9. A month is always…

    a. 31 days long.

    b. 30 days long.

    c. 29 days long.

    d. 28, 29, 30, or 31 days long.

10. Traders _____ things to people.

    a. give

    b. mean

    c. sell

    d. remember

Let's Read More!

Time

1   The calendar and the clock measure time. A clock shows the 24 hours of a day—12 in the morning and 12 in the evening. The word *minute* means "small." So parts of an hour are small measures of time, minutes. A minute has
5   60 parts too. These are the "second" small measures of time. We call them *seconds*. Think about it: small (*minute*) and a "second" kind of small.

Let's Practice!

A. *True* or *False*?

Write *true* or *false* in each blank.

1. _____ Calendars have numbers on them.

2. _____ A number on a calendar is a symbol.

3. _____ There are 54 weeks in a year.

4. _____ A farm is a person.

5. _____   One kind of plant is a flower.

6. _____   There are 60 seconds in a minute.

7. _____   A seller is a trader.

8. _____   A full moon looks like a circle.

B. Find the Different Word

One word in each group is different. Circle it. How is it different from the other words? How are the other words like one another?

1. summer	spring	winter	fall	star
2. farmer	about	king	man of the church	
3. season	know	week	year	day
4. month	moon	sun	star	
5. second	minute	first	day	hour
6. picture	black	blue	red	

C. Find Other Words with These Meanings

Find a word or phrase with a similar meaning.

1. days, hours, minutes, seconds = _____

2. symbol = _____

3. January and June = _____

4. spring, summer, fall, and winter = _____

5. small = _____

D. Pictures Are Symbols

A picture of a person and a book means "library." The picture is not a library. It is a symbol. A picture of a flower or a star can be a symbol too. A heart is a symbol of love.

Many symbols are easy to write. They are not pictures of people or things. They are little marks.

Here are a few symbols. You can find them in many places. Do you know their meanings?

$ means   _____

c/o   means   _____

\#   means   _____

\+   means   _____

\=   means   _____

%   means   _____

@   means   _____

&   means   _____

Do you know any other symbols? Draw them for your classmates. Tell their meanings.

Symbols

Let's Read More!

The Moon

1   People watched the moon and the stars. They learned about the sun, too. They made up stories about the stars, the sun, and the moon. There are many interesting stories about the moon. The moon seems like a face. The face is
5   the "man in the moon." And there are funny things about the moon. For example, more babies are born under a full moon. The moon in October seems very big and yellow. It has a special name—the harvest moon. It makes people feel quiet and happy. It looks full and rich, like the food
10   brought from the fields.

    There is another story about the moon. A year has thirteen full moons. In some months there are two full moons. A second full moon in a month is a "blue moon." There are not many blue moons. So *once in a blue moon*
15   means "not often." Unusual things happen in a blue moon. (Well, that's what people say.)

Let's Learn from the Reading!

Answer these questions about the reading.

1. Who is the man in the moon?
   - a. a real person
   - b. a face on the moon
   - c. a farmer
   - d. a blue moon

2. When do we have a harvest moon?
   - a. spring
   - b. summer
   - c. fall
   - d. winter

3. *Once in a blue moon* means...

    a. pictures

    b. the man in the moon.

    c. not very often.

    d. changes in the seasons.

 Let's Talk!

Talk with a classmate. Here are some ideas.

1. A farmer needs records. Many years ago, a farmer made marks on a stick with a knife. Each mark meant a measure of food from the fields. That stick was like a record book. As business people, traders kept records of selling and buying. They made spots, or marks, on sticks too.

   Today we have other ways to keep records. What are some of them? Do you keep records? How?

2. Do you know a story about the moon? If you do, tell the story.

 Let's Do More!

Do you drive a car? Do you ride a bicycle? Do you ride the bus? Of course, you use the roads. There are many symbols to help drivers. They are important for people on the roads.

1. What do these symbols mean?

    a.  a stop sign (red) _____

    b.  a diamond (white and yellow) _____

    c.  a traffic light (red, yellow, and green) _____

2. Can you think of other traffic signs? Make a list of symbols on the streets and roads.

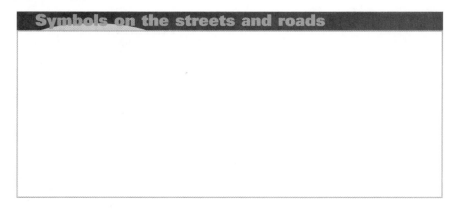

 Let's Write!

Use these questions to write about the year. First read the questions with your class. Then answer the questions. Write all the answers in sentences on the lines. The answers to the questions will make a paragraph. Write your name on the blank after "by."

How many seasons are there in a year?

What is the first season?
What are some signs of this season?

What is the second season?
What are some signs of this season?

Which season comes next?
What are some signs of this season?

What is the last season of the year?
What are some signs of this season?

About the Year

by _____

_____

_____

_____

_____

_____

_____

_____

_____

_____

_____

_____

_____

_____

_____

_____

_____

_____

_____

Let's Find Out About You!

1. When were you born? (month, date, year)

2. In which season were you born?

Plateau I
Around Our World

Before You Read

1. Look at the first picture.

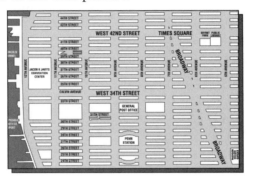

This is a part of a _____ .

The lines are _____ .

This map is useful for travelers.

2. What is in picture #2?

There are _____ people.
(Use a number.)

They are looking at globes.

The globe has the shape of a ball.

The globe is a map of the Earth.

It shows oceans and continents.

One ocean is the Atlantic Ocean.

Another is the Pacific.

Do you know the names of other oceans?

There are seven continents.

Continents are large land plates.

Point out the continents you see in the picture.

Asia and Africa are continents.

Between Africa and Europe is the Mediterranean Sea.

Can you find it? Can you find other seas?

How are oceans and seas different from each other?

---

3. The third picture is also a map.

The map has little symbols on it. These symbols mean the products of the area. What does each symbol mean? Can you guess?

What does mean?

What does mean?

What does mean?

What does mean?

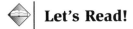 **Let's Read!**

Our Home World

1   The Earth is our home. We all live here. The Earth is like our mother and father. The Earth gives everything to us. The Earth gives us food. It gives us shelter. *Shelter* means "a place safe from the weather."

5   We need shelter from snow and ice. We need shelter from the rain and the sun. We need air and water, too. There is air for us all around the Earth. The Earth holds the air for us. Our planet has lots of water. One name for Earth is "the Water Planet." Because of the air and the

10 water, we can live here.

    The Earth takes care of us. We must also take care of the Earth. We study about the Earth for this reason. Geography is the study of the Earth. There are many parts to the study of geography. It is the study

15 of rivers, oceans, and mountains. Geography includes the study of animals and plants. It is the study of weather and climate, too.

20   Many people study geography. They want to learn about the Earth. They find out about the resources of the Earth.

25   Natural resources are useful things from the Earth. Some of these resources are metals, coal, and oil. We go into the Earth to get them.

A geographer learns about the borders of countries. Borders are lines between countries. Geographers learn about cities, too. Geographers also learn about history. They learn about people and about different ways of life. Are borders important? You walk across a border, and you look at the people. Are the people different? Of course, in different countries, people have different ideas. Many countries have languages of their own.

The cultures of different countries are special to them. For example, religion makes a big difference. In the Middle East and parts of Asia and Africa, there are many Muslims. The people follow Muslim customs. Europe, North America, and South America are mostly Christian. The religion is the Christian religion. In the Far East some of the great religions are Buddhism, Hinduism, and Shintoism. Many customs come from religion.

Geography is really interesting to study because one learns about so many things. People learn about the Earth and all of its people. Studying geography does another good thing. People study geography, and they learn to understand one another.

≈ | Let's Learn from the Reading!

Here are some questions about the reading. Can you answer them? If you can, then you understand the reading.

1. Why is the Earth our home?
   a. We live here on the Earth.
   b. Geographers study the Earth.
   c. There are many different countries on the Earth.
   d. The Earth has many resources.

2. How is the Earth like a mother and father?

    a. The Earth has many cultures.

    b. People have different ideas.

    c. The Earth gives us necessary things.

    d. We need shelter from the weather.

3. Where is there always a border?

    a. in a city   c. between countries

    b. near rivers   d. in the mountains

4. Why is it good to study geography?

    a. We learn about geographers and history.

    b. We study rivers and oceans.

    c. We learn about people and their cultures.

    d. We study our resources and the animals.

5. What are the names of some world religions?

    _____ _____ _____

    _____ _____

Let's Practice!

A. What Do Geographers Do?

Does a geographer…? (Circle *yes* or *no*.)

1. study rivers	yes	no
2. study the Earth's history	yes	no
3. look at maps	yes	no
4. buy products on maps	yes	no
5. study countries and their borders	yes	no
6. learn about resources	yes	no
7. learn about animals and plants	yes	no
8. study cultures of different people	yes	no
9. study oceans	yes	no
10. find natural resources	yes	no

B. Natural Resources

Circle the names of natural resources.

rivers	weather	animals
water	continents	oceans
plants	products	climate
cars	culture	oil
coal	shelter	seas
metal	borders	air

 Let's Talk!

First answer the questions for yourself. Then talk with a classmate about your answers.

1. Coal, oil, and metal are some resources. Do you know some other important resources? Make a list: _____

   _____

2. How far do you live from a border? _____

3. How much change does a border make between the people on both sides? _____

4. What part of the study of geography do you like? _____

5. What does this sentence mean? "Understanding brings peace."

   _____

Let's Read More!

Variety on the Earth

1   Who lives on the Earth? Human beings and animals do. Human beings are people. The Earth has people of different kinds, shapes, and sizes. Some people are tall. Others are short. The skin of some people is dark. Some
5   have light skin. Some have dark hair. Other people are blond. Some people have curly hair. Other people's hair is straight. What a variety!

The Earth has different climates, too. For example, there are hot places and cold places. People can live in all
10   kinds of climates. Some people live in hot places easily. Others live in cold areas easily. The cold weather is not bad for their health. Cold climate fits them. It is right for them. But hot weather is not. It is not easy for these people to live in hot climates.

15   Eskimos are a good example. Their families live in the cold North. They live in a cold climate. The snow and ice are natural to them. They do not mind the cold. Modern Eskimos live in houses, and they buy some of their food. But it is very expensive. There are not many plants in the
20   North. And there are no farms in very cold climates.

So, Eskimos do not eat much food from plants. They eat fish from the ocean, and they hunt for meat. Eskimos do not have much variety of food, but they are healthy.

Eskimos' land has a lot of snow and ice. The light of
25   the sun on the snow and ice is very bright. Bright light does not usually hurt dark eyes. The Eskimos have dark eyes. They also have dark skin. The dark skin and eyes keep them safe from the sun. The Eskimos are the people
30   of the snow areas. They are the right people to live there.

All parts of the world are not the same. People do not all look the same, either. The people of the South are different from the people of the North. The people of the hot areas of the world could not live in cold climate, either. In some
35   places there is little water. The people there are usually small. The people from dry areas are different from the people from wet areas.

North, South, East, and West—there is a lot of variety on Earth. The parts of the Earth are different. Of course, the
40   people from different parts of the world are different too!

Let's Learn from the Reading!

Here are some questions for you. They are about the reading. Do you understand the reading?

1. Who lives on the Earth? _____

2. What keeps Eskimos safe from the bright light of the sun?
   a. dark skin
   b. dark hair
   c. light skin
   d. light eyes

3. Eskimos eat a lot of…
   a. plants.
   b. fish.
   c. snow.
   d. ice.

4. People do not all look the same. How are people different?

   _____

5. Why does the Earth have a variety of people?
   a. People don't fit all climates. So, the weather is different in many areas.
   b. Climates are different. So, there are different foods on the Earth.
   c. There is a variety of foods. So, there is different weather for each food.
   d. There is a variety of climates. People are different in each climate.

Let's Practice!

A. *True* or *False?*

Write *true* or *false* in each blank.

1. _____ Eskimos are blond.

2. _____ Eskimos have dark eyes.

3. _____ All Eskimos look the same.

4. _____ Eskimos do not eat much food from plants.

5. _____ Eskimos live in a warm climate.

6. _____ Eskimos live in houses now.

B. Fill in the Blanks

1. North is the name of one of the four directions. The others are

   _____ , _____ , and _____ .

2. There are seven continents. Australia and Antarctica are big islands in the South.

   The other continents are:

   _____ _____ _____

   _____ _____

3. One great ocean is the Atlantic. The other big ocean is the

   _____ .

C. One Is the Same as the Other

Sometimes two people look the same. They have the same mother. They have the same birthday. Joan and Jane are twins. Joan and Jane look the same.

1. Fill in the blanks. Complete the sentences.

     a. Their hair is _____ _____ color.

     b. They have _____ _____ shape.

     c. They even like _____ _____ foods.

2. Look at their picture. Read the questions.
   Which answer is right?
   Circle Answer A or Answer B.

     a. Are the twins tall?

        Answer A: Yes, they are.

        Answer B: No, they aren't.

     b. Are the twins short?

        Answer A: Yes, they are.

        Answer B: No, they aren't.

     c. Do the twins have curly hair?

        Answer A: Yes, they do.

        Answer B: No, they don't.

     d. Do the twins look the same?

        Answer A: Yes, they do.

        Answer B: No, they don't.

     e. Are they the same size?

        Answer A: Yes, they are.

        Answer B: No, they aren't.

     f. Do they have the same shape?

        Answer A: Yes, they do.

        Answer B: No, they don't.

Let's Talk!

First read the questions. Think about your own answers first, and then talk with a classmate.

1. How does it help someone to learn about people in other parts of the world?

2. What facts about the world's geography make a difference in climate?

3. Another word for *variety* is *diversity*. How does diversity in people and ideas make a country strong?

Let's Read More!

Two Different Ways of Life

1   There are four necessary things for life. They are air, water, food, and shelter. Everyone breathes air. Everyone drinks water. These two things are the same for everybody every place. But there are different ways of life. Ways to get

5   food, water, and shelter are different.

Here are two examples:

Family A lives in a small village. They have a simple house. In this village, people get water from the river. They get fish, too. Every family has a garden. The women

10   and the children take care of the gardens. The men go hunting for meat. These families do not use much money. They have a simple way of life. They do not need the cities. They can live without many other people near them.

Family B lives in a city. Mr. and Mrs. B have jobs. They

15   earn money. They use the money to pay for necessary things. For example, they buy all of their food. They pay for water. They buy their clothes with money. They pay for their home. Family B's life is not very simple. They need

other people around them. They give money to these other

20   people for necessary things.

The two families have different customs. These customs make their lives very different. Perhaps they have different languages, too. Language and customs make up a culture. Culture is a way of life. All over the world, there are different

25   ways of life, so we can talk about different cultures.

≈ | Let's Learn from the Reading!

Find the answers to this question in the reading.

What are the necessary things for life? _____

_____ _____ _____

◎ | Let's Practice!

A. *True or False?*

Write *true* or *false* in each blank.

1. _____ Family A has a simple way of life.

2. _____ Family B has a simple way of life.

3. _____ In a simple way of life, money is necessary.

4. _____ Fish live in a river.

5. _____ Four things necessary for life are air, food, language, and culture.

B. Why Do We Need Language?

Human beings need language. Why? Put an X in front of each reason for language.

1. _____ to talk to one another

2. _____ to have a simple way of life

3. _____ to get necessary things

4. _____ to breathe air

5. _____ to live with animals

6. _____ to learn more about the world

7. _____ to help other people

8. _____ to read books

9. _____ to talk about ideas

10. _____ to play games

◇ Let's Talk!

Think about these questions. Then talk with a friend. Are your answers the same as your friend's answers? How are they different? Why?

1. What is your way of life?

    a. How is it simple?

    b. How is it NOT simple?

2. How do you get the necessary things for life?

3. Which ones are free? (*Free* means "at no cost.")

    a. Is food free?

    b. Is water free?

    c. Is air free?

    d. Is the weather free?

    e. Is shelter free?

4. What are some customs in your family?

5. English is a language. What are some other languages?

6. What do you use language to do?

Let's Read More!

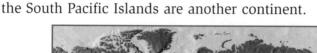

1   What is a continent? A continent is a large piece of land. Another name is *land mass*. How many continents are there? There are seven continents. The names of the continents are Africa, Antarctica, Asia, Australia, Europe,
5   North America, and South America. To some geographers, the South Pacific Islands are another continent.

     What makes a continent? Far under the ground, the Earth is very hot rock. The rock there is liquid, like thick water. The continents do not all look like separate lands.

10   On a map, for example, Africa, Asia, and Europe look like one big piece of land. But are they? No, they are not. They simply touch one another. Each continent is like a separate, solid island on the hot liquid rock in the Earth. These "islands" are plates. Each continent is a separate
15   plate. Sometimes these plates move. The solid plates move on the liquid rock. Then there is an earthquake.

     Australia and Antarctica are really large islands. Antarctica is at the South Pole. Snow and ice cover the South Pole. But there is land under the thick cover of ice.
20   How big is the land of Antarctica? No one really knows.

≈| Let's Learn from the Reading!

Fill in the blanks with answers from the reading.

1. What are the names of the continents?

   _____ _____

   _____ _____

   _____ _____

   _____

2. Which continents touch one another?

   a. _____ and _____

   b. _____ , _____ , and

      _____

3. Which continents are islands in the oceans?

   _____ and _____

4. Why is Europe a separate continent from Asia?

   a. They don't have the same culture, so their languages are different.

   b. Asia and Europe are separate plates. They only touch each other.

   c. Australia is between Europe and Asia, so they cannot touch each other.

   d. Europe and Asia don't like the same food, so they have separate plates.

Let's Read More!

Water Planet

1   Earth is the Water Planet. Water covers 70% (seventy percent) of the Earth. Water covers many parts of the Earth. There are names for these parts. Between the Americas and Europe and Africa is the Atlantic Ocean. The Pacific

5   Ocean is west of the American continents. The Pacific is the world's largest ocean. South of India is the Indian Ocean. The Arctic Ocean is a small ocean near the North Pole. We call some parts of the water seas, not oceans. Between South and North America is the Caribbean Sea.

10   The North Sea is between Great Britain and North Europe. The China Sea is near China. Near Alaska is the Bering Sea. The Mediterranean Sea is between Europe and Africa. The Baltic Sea is in the middle of some northern European countries. The Red Sea is between Africa and Arabia. The

15   Black Sea is north of Turkey in the western part of Asia.

    Some seas are like very big lakes. The largest sea is the Caspian Sea, in Iran. There is land all around the Caspian Sea. And there are some other large lakes. These seas have fresh water. That is water without much salt. Lake Baikal is

20   a freshwater lake in Siberia. Lake Victoria is in Africa, and Great Bear Lake is in Canada. The Great Lakes (five lakes) of North America are between Canada and the United States. It's easy to understand why this is the Water Planet.

Let's Learn from the Reading!

Look at the reading again, and then answer these questions or fill in the blanks.

1. The water between the Americas and Europe-Africa is...

    a. the Atlantic Sea.

    b. the Pacific Ocean.

    c. the Red Ocean.

    d. the Atlantic Ocean.

    e. the Pacific Sea.

    f. the Mediterranean Sea.

2. What is the name of the body of water between Africa and Europe?

    a. the Atlantic Ocean

    b. the Pacific Ocean

    c. the Red Sea

    d. the Mediterranean Sea

    e. the South Sea

    f. the Baltic Sea

3. Lake Victoria is in _____ .

4. The _____ _____ are between Canada and the United States.

5. The Bering Sea _____ near _____ .

Let's Read More!

Mountains

1　　The Earth has mountains on every continent. Most mountains are parts of groups. A mountain group is "a mountain range." There are many high mountains, but the highest mountains are the Himalayas in Asia. Next are
5　the Andes, in South America. In North America, the high mountains are the Rockies and the Sierras. Africa has the Atlas Mountains in the north. Europe has the Alps. Australia has some mountains too. But they are small. The South Pacific has mountains too, but these mountains
10　are islands. The ocean in the South Pacific is very deep. Only the tops of the mountains are above water. These mountaintop islands are called Micronesia.

 Let's Practice!

Draw a line from each mountain to its continent.

1. Andes	a. Europe
2. Atlas	b. South Pacific
3. Alps	c. Asia
4. Himalayas	d. South America
5. Rockies	e. Africa
6. Micronesia	f. North America

 **Let's Read More!**

Great Rivers of the World

1   There are many great rivers in our world. The Amazon
River is the biggest. It is in South America. It is called "the
river sea." At most places, a person cannot see from one
side to the other. It is too far! No other river in the world
5   is this large. The river begins in the west of South America
and ends in the east. It begins high in the Andes Mountains
and runs across Brazil and into the Atlantic Ocean.

The greatest river of Africa is the Nile River. The Nile
is an important river in Africa. Most of Egypt is very dry.
10   It is a desert. So, in Egypt, the Nile is the life-giver. (It gives
life to the fields, to the people, to the animals.) To the south,
Africa also has parts that are very wet. The Congo and the
Zambezi rivers are in these parts of Africa. These rivers
are in the heart of the continent.

15   Asia also has great rivers. For example, there is the
Ganges in India. The Yangtze is in Tibet and in China.
These rivers—like the Nile in Egypt—are working rivers.
People use them for travel. In Asia many people live in
boats on the rivers. The rivers have fish for the people to
20   eat. The rivers give water for the farms, too.

The largest river in North America is the Mississippi.
Two other great rivers add their water to the Mississippi;
they are the Ohio and the Missouri. Together, these rivers
make a great water road for transportation. Between
25   Canada and the United States is the Saint Lawrence River.
It is a road to the sea through the Great Lakes. In North
America, in Canada, and in the north part of the United
States, there are other large rivers. In the summer, the

30 Mackenzie and the Yukon are popular for sports. They are open in the summer, but the snow and ice of winter close them for more than half of the year.

Europe has important rivers too. The Rhine, the Thames, the Neva, the Seine, the Danube, and the Rhone are some of them. All of these rivers are working rivers.
35 They are water roads across a continent.

 Let's Practice!

Read quickly to find the answers to the exercise. Where is each of these rivers? Draw a line from each river to the name of the continent.

1. Amazon
2. Nile
3. Seine   a. Africa
4. Rhine
5. Conga
6. Yangtze   b. Europe
7. Neva
8. Thames
9. Ganges   c. North America
10. Danube
11. Mackenzie
12. St. Lawrence   d. South America
13. Rhone
14. Mississippi
15. Zambezi   e. Asia
16. Missouri
17. Yukon
18. Ohio

Let's Talk!

Think about these sentences. What are your ideas? Talk with a classmate about your ideas and his or her ideas. Do you both agree? (Do the two of you think the same way?)

1. The world is one big village.
2. On Earth no person is really alone.
3. No person is an island.
4. Rivers are like people.
5. There are mountains, so some people want to go to the tops of them.

 ## Let's Find Out About You!

Answer these questions and then talk about them with a classmate.

1. Describe yourself. What words fit you? _____

   _____

2. Where on Earth are you?

   What is north of you? _____

   What is south of you? _____

   What is to the east of you? _____

   What is to the west of you? _____

3. What climate fits you best? Why? _____

   _____

Step 6

Before You Read

1. How is life different in a city and on a farm?

2. Where are there more people?

3. A city has more people than a small town or a farm community. Does this fact mean more friends for a city person? Why or why not?

4. How can a person meet new people? And where?

Alone in a Crowd

1   Many people live alone, and they live far from home. They don't live with their families. Why? There are many good reasons. Some of these people are students. They must leave home. They go away for college. Most of them

5   study at college for four years. Some study for five or six! Then they leave college. Usually they go to different cities. They look for jobs. They find jobs in a city, so they live in that city. They must live near their work.

Some of these people are far from home. Some people

10   go to cities alone. They have no friends in the city. They don't know people. Perhaps their families live many miles away. Sometimes cities are not friendly places. People can be alone in a crowd. There may be many people around them, but they feel alone.

15   Perhaps they live in small apartments in big buildings. There are a lot of people in such a building. For example, there are people across the hall—in another apartment. Yet apartment houses are not friendly places. Most people in apartments don't know other people in their building.

20   They may be neighbors, but they are not friends. People may want to find friends, but they don't look for them in apartment buildings. People living close together want to make their own area seem larger. Not knowing their neighbors gives them that feeling.

25   Yet they want and need others. What can they do? They can look for ways to make new friends. But where can they find friends? Perhaps they find them at work. Perhaps they find friends in other places. Some people find friends with the same religion. They can go to churches, mosques, and

30   temples to meet others. Some people find friends in schools.

They want to meet people, so they take classes at schools at night. Other people go to social clubs. They can meet new people there. They talk. Maybe they enjoy card games. Perhaps they even learn to dance.

35   Other people find friends through sports. Perhaps they go to watch sports. Some like to play sports. Maybe they want to swim. So they will look for a swimming pool. Or perhaps they play tennis. They look for other tennis players. Golf players go to a country club. There they can find 40   friends. They meet people in this way. They have new friends, so they are not alone anymore. A person can make new friends. However, the person must work at it! Then the crowd can be a large group of friends.

Let's Learn from the Reading!

Do you know the answers to these questions? Look at the reading again—if you need to.

1. How long do students usually study at college?

    a. one year   c. two years

    b. three years   d. four years

2. What is a job?

    a. It is work.   c. It is a home.

    b. It is a city.   d. It is college.

3. What is the main idea of "Alone in a Crowd"?

    a. People can find new friends in big cities.

    b. Some people live with their families.

    c. Families and friends are at college.

    d. Students at college learn a lot.

4. People live in the city. Perhaps they study there. There is another reason. What is it?

   a. Their friends are in the city.

   b. They don't know others in the city.

   c. They don't like farms.

   d. Their jobs are in the city.

5. Which sentence is in "Alone in a Crowd"? Find the sentence in the reading and underline it.

   a. Perhaps they find friends in other places.

   b. People live near other people in apartment buildings.

   c. Some people are alone with many people around them.

   d. Some people like to play cards at social clubs.

6. Where do many people in cities live?

   a. in apartment buildings

   b. near the middle of the city

   c. on the main street

   d. at sports clubs

7. Where can people find friends in a city? (Circle all the right answers.)

   a. at a swimming pool

   b. at night school

   c. in social clubs

   d. on the street

   e. at work

   f. at their jobs

   g. at a golf club

   h. in apartment buildings

   i. at a sports game

   j. at a college

   k. in different cities

   l. at churches, temples, and mosques

8. A _____ lives in a house or apartment near you.
    a. neighbor   c. crowd
    b. friend   d. player

9. An apartment is in a...
    a. church.   c. club.
    b. building.   d. city.

10. A person can _____ new friends.
    a. watch   c. make
    b. be alone with   d. leave

11. A crowd is like...
    a. a place to live.
    b. a place to learn.
    c. a large group of people.
    d. a family.

12. Where do people play cards? People play cards...
    a. at school.
    b. far away.
    c. in apartments.
    d. at social clubs.

Let's Practice!

A. *True* or *False*?

Write *true* or *false* in each blank.

1. _____ City people sometimes go to churches to meet new people.

2. _____ People can learn to play cards at social clubs.

3. _____ There are many apartments in one building.

4. _____ There are lonely people in a city.

5. _____ Many students leave home to go to college.

6. _____ In a city you cannot be alone in a crowd.

7. _____ An apartment building has apartments in it.

8. _____ Temples and mosques are buildings for sports.

9. _____ A social club is a school.

10. _____ There are no clubs for golf players.

11. _____ You can go to school at night.

12. _____ Your neighbors are always your friends.

B. Find the Different Word

One word in each group is different from the other words. Find it. Draw a circle around it. How is it different from the others? How are the other words like one another?

1.	perhaps	usually	always	might	often
2.	families	friends	people	cities	
3.	apartment	building	house	home	card
4.	different	people	alone	big	
5.	four	first	six	five	
6.	and	the	but	yet	
7.	social	know	study	live	meet
8.	around	from	no	in	to
9.	many	some	alone	other	
10.	these	them	this	the	a
11.	friendly	hospital	college	church	library
12.	students	near	away	far	

Let's Read More!

Volunteer!

1   Help other people, and you make friends. Help other people, and you feel good. Helping can make you healthy! It's true! Doctors often study things like this. Their studies show it! Volunteers are always welcome. A volunteer does
5   a job for no money. To do work for free is to volunteer.

Do you want to be a volunteer? You can volunteer for just two or three hours a week. What can you do? You can take care of a neighbor's child. You stay with the child and watch him or her. You can play with the child. Then the mother or
10   father will have some free time. Perhaps then a busy parent can go shopping. Sometimes parents need time alone.

You can volunteer to take care of an old person. Perhaps you can take an old person for a walk. Or, you can read to an old person, or write letters for him or her.

15   You can work at a special home for homeless children. Many volunteers work with hurt children. These children always need someone to talk to them. They need someone to read stories to them. They want someone to play with them. You can go to a children's hospital to talk or read
20   stories to the children. Children in hospitals enjoy that very much. You can help in a hospital.

You can be a volunteer in a school, too. You can be a volunteer at a soup kitchen. Homeless people can get food there. Many good neighbors work in soup kitchens in cities.
25   They give food to hungry people who are alone in a crowd.

It is good to be a volunteer. You can learn a lot about your new city. You can meet people. You can do something for others. And you feel good, too.

Let's Learn from the Reading!

Read the questions and try to answer them. Talk with a friend from the class. Are your answers the same as your classmate's?

1. What does *to volunteer* mean?
    a. to work with friends
    b. to work for no money
    c. to help people
    d. to read to children

2. A good way to meet people is to…
    a. volunteer.
    b. eat at a soup kitchen.
    c. write letters.
    d. play games for two or three hours a week.

3. Children without a place to live are _____ children.
    a. home
    b. homeless
    c. volunteer
    d. hurt

4. Where can a volunteer work? (Circle all the right answers.)
    a. at a library
    b. in a school
    c. at a church
    d. in a hospital
    e. at a golf club
    f. at a soup kitchen
    g. in a college class
    h. at a home for homeless children
    i. at a home for old people

◎ | Let's Practice!

A. *True* or *False?*

Write *true* or *false* in each blank.

1. _____   Homeless people do not have homes.

2. _____   Homeless people work in soup kitchens.

3. _____   Homeless people can eat in soup kitchens.

4. _____   Volunteers can work in hospitals.

5. _____   Some old people cannot write letters without help.

6. _____   There are children in some hospitals.

7. _____   Volunteers feel good about their work.

8. _____   There are special homes for homeless children.

B. Find the Same Meaning

Draw a line between the two words or phrases with similar meanings.

1. for no money   a. stay to watch someone

2. feel good   b. neighbor

3. do something for others   c. type of work for money

4. volunteer   d. do work for no money

5. take care of someone   e. be healthy

6. job   f. for free

7. person who lives nearby   g. help people

C. Find Other Words with These Meanings

Find a word or phrase with a similar meaning.

1. job = _____

2. have fun = _____

3. go away = _____

4. look for = _____

5. perhaps = _____

6. family = _____

Let's Talk!

Talk with a friend about the answers to these questions.

1. Do you live near some big cities? What are they?
2. Do you know the name of a big city? What is it?
3. What is the biggest city near your home?
4. Do you live in a city now? (If so, when did you come to the city? When did you arrive?)
5. Do you live on a farm now? (Perhaps you don't live on a farm now. Did you ever live on a farm?)
6. Do you live in a small town now? (If you do not now, did you ever?)

Let's Write!

Big cities are sometimes lonely places, but big cities are fun, too. Many people visit cities to have fun. There are many interesting things to do in a city. What are some of them? Write them in the blanks.

Cities

_____

_____

_____

_____

_____

_____

_____

_____

_____

_____

_____

_____

_____

_____

Let's Find Out About You!

Almost every person sometimes feels alone. What do you do to change that feeling?

Step 7

Before You Read

1. Some people understand others and their problems well.
   They can help others find answers to their problems.
   These understanding people have the gift of wisdom.
   They are wise people. Wise people make good teachers.
   Explain *wisdom*.

2. It is easy to understand a problem and a solution or
   answer to the problem in a story. Do you know a story
   that is also a lesson? Tell others about the story.

3. Are stories good lessons? Why or why not?

Aesop, a Man of Wisdom

Aesop lived many years ago. His country was Greece. Aesop understood people very well.

He was a wise and intelligent man. He had the gift of wisdom. Aesop told stories with lessons in them. They were clever stories! We have a special name for Aesop's stories. We call them fables.

Most fables are animal stories. Fables teach lessons. A fable lesson is a moral. The moral of a story teaches the difference between good and bad.

The Greeks learned important life lessons from Aesop's fables. They liked his stories. They told his fables again and again. Aesop's fables became familiar to almost everyone. People still like Aesop's fables. Parents tell his stories to their children. Today people learn from Aesop too. Everyone enjoys these fables.

Here is one of Aesop's famous fables. It is about a crow and a fox. A crow is a bird. It is large and black, and not very pretty. Crows make a sound, but it is not a nice song! A fox is an animal. Most foxes are clever animals. The fox in this story is very clever too!

THE FOX AND THE CROW

One beautiful day, a fox saw a crow up in a tree. There was food in her mouth. The fox was hungry and wanted that food. So he sat under the tree. He waited, and he watched. He looked at the food. The fox thought and thought. He wanted the crow's food for lunch. Then he had an idea.

The fox said, "Hello, Ms. Crow. You are a beautiful bird. Do you have a beautiful voice, too? Do you sing well?"

The crow did not think. She was not clever like the
10 fox. She opened her mouth.

She wanted to sing for the fox. (Crows don't know that they don't sing well!) She opened her mouth, and the food fell. It dropped from her mouth. The food fell down to the fox. The fox opened his mouth. The food fell in. Then the
15 fox ran away. He did not wait to hear the crow's song. It wasn't a pretty song anyway.

That fox was intelligent. He understood the crow very well. What do you think about the
20 fox? Did he really want to hear the crow's voice? Did he want the crow to sing for him? Did he truly think that the crow was beautiful? What is the moral of this fable? What lesson does the story teach?

≃| Let's Learn from the Reading!

1. Where did Aesop live? _____

2. What is a moral?
   a. a bit of food
   b. a large fox
   c. a lesson
   d. a beautiful voice

3. What is the reading "Aesop, a Man of Wisdom" about?

   a. Foxes talk.

   b. Fables are about animals.

   c. Aesop's fables teach lessons.

   d. People like Aesop's fables a lot.

4. The fox asked, "Do you sing well?" What did he want?
   He wanted...

   a. to hear a story.   c. to sing a song.

   b. the crow's food.   d. to sing for the crow.

5. Which sentence is in "Aesop, a Man of Wisdom"? (Find the
   sentence in the reading and underline it.)

   a. The Greeks told Aesop's stories to their children.

   b. People today like fables and other stories.

   c. The Greeks learned lessons from Aesop's fables.

   d. The fox was hungry and wanted that food.

6. Where was the crow? _____

7. What did the fox eat?

   a. morals   c. fables

   b. a bit of food   d. the crow

8. What is a fable?

   a. It is a lesson in a song.

   b. It is usually a story about animals.

   c. It is a wise and intelligent man from Greece.

   d. It is a beautiful voice.

9. What color is a crow? _____

10. What is the moral of this fable?

    a. Eat food from other people's mouths.

    b. Don't sing for other people.

    c. Clever people can take things from you.

    d. Clever people like food, not songs.

Let's Practice!

A. *True* or *False?*

Write *true* or *false* in each blank.

1. _____ A Greek man by the name of Aesop told clever stories.

2. _____ Animals use stories to teach children.

3. _____ The fox is a wise animal.

4. _____ One big black bird is a fox.

5. _____ Aesop was Greek.

6. _____ Aesop was a great teacher.

7. _____ The fox dropped the food.

8. _____ Foxes like fables.

9. _____ People still enjoy Aesop's stories today.

10. _____ Crows are clever birds with beautiful voices.

11. _____ Greek people are from Greece.

12. _____ *Clever* and *wise* have similar meanings.

B. Find the Different Word

One word in the group is different from the other words. Can you find it? Draw a circle around it. How is the word different from the others? How are the others alike?

1. intelligent   wisdom   clever

2. mouth   story   fable

3. song   drop   sell   fall

4. animal   lesson   moral

5. under   about   his   in   at

6. intelligent   clever   voice

7. sang   like   saw   sat

8.	ago	the	an	a
9.	them	their	they	the
10.	food	good	bad	
11.	crow	tree	fox	bird
12.	intelligent	clever	pretty	wise

 Let's Read More!

Aesop wrote many fables. He wrote a fable about a goose.

THE GOOSE AND HER GOLD EGGS

1   A man owned a fine goose. She was a wonderful bird. Every day she gave the man a gift of an egg. These eggs were special. They were gold. But the goose gave only one golden egg a day.

5   Yet the man was not happy. He wanted more. He wanted many golden eggs a day. He wanted a lot of gold. The man was greedy.

10 He wanted all the gold from the goose, and he wanted it right away. He was not able to wait.

    What did the man do? He

15 wanted to look inside the goose. So, he did a bad thing.

    What did he do? He killed the big beautiful white bird. Then he looked inside. But there was no gold there. There was no gold in the goose. There was nothing there at all. His special goose was just a goose.

What is the moral of this story?

a. Don't kill a goose.

b. Don't be greedy.

c. There is no gold in a goose.

d. Don't look inside a big bird.

Aesop wrote another fable. This story was about a mountain.

THE MOUSE AND THE MOUNTAIN

1   One day a mountain made a lot of noise. The mountain moaned. It cried. The people said, "The mountain will have a baby." Then the people waited. The noise was very loud. The people were afraid. But they waited and waited.

5   They watched the mountain. At last, the mountain sighed. The noise stopped. What was it? What came from the mountain? Then the mountain sighed again. A small mouse came out.

What is the lesson of this fable?

a. Some people have small problems, but they cry a lot.

b. A loud noise can be a small problem.

c. Don't talk to big people. They moan a lot.

d. Big people, like mountains, have many problems. So, they sigh a lot.

Let's Practice!

Find Other Words with These Meanings

Find a word or phrase with a similar meaning.

1. clever = _____

2. a moral = _____

3. cried = _____

4. dropped = _____

5. animal stories with lessons in them = _____

6. a large black bird = _____

◇ Let's Talk!

1. Do you know any other fables? What are some of them? Tell another classmate a story with a moral.

2. Wisdom is one special gift. What are some other gifts that some people have?

3. What are your gifts?

◇ Let's Write!

Proverbs are lessons in one sentence. People make sayings from fables. People use these one-line sayings often. These sayings are proverbs. Here are some proverbs. Why do people say them? What do these proverbs mean?

1. Don't kill the goose that lays the golden egg.

   _____

2. It's a lot of noise about nothing.

   _____

3. Don't let someone's nice words trick you.

   _____

4. The cat is away, so the mice play.

   _____

5. Don't cry over spilled milk.

   _____

6. Don't worry about yesterday. Think about tomorrow.

   _____

Let's Read Some More Fables!

Here are four more short stories for you. They are all stories about birds. Read each story, and then ask yourself the questions.

1. A bird was looking for food in the water. He found some little plants to eat, but he didn't want them. The plants floated away down the river. Then he found some tiny fish. But they were too small. These fish swam behind a rock. Then he found a bigger fish, but it wasn't big enough. He let the fish go. Then the bird looked and looked, but he couldn't find anything to eat.

    a. Is this story a fable? _____

    b. Does it teach a lesson? _____

    c. What is the moral of this story? _____

    _____

2. One day a chicken was out in the forest. A little nut fell from a tree. It was hard and small. It hit the head of the chicken. "Ouch!" said the bird. Then the bird looked around. What had fallen? He looked down on the ground. But he didn't see the nut. Then he looked around, and he saw nothing. Next he looked up, and what did he see? The sky! This chicken was not very intelligent, and he didn't understand. What fell on his head and hurt him? It must be the sky! "Oh, oh!" cried the chicken. "The sky is falling." The chicken ran to all his friends. He shouted the news to them, "The sky is falling!" His friends were afraid too. They ran to tell other friends. Soon everyone was afraid.

    a. Is this story a fable? _____

    b. Does it teach a lesson? _____

    c. What is the moral of this story? _____

    _____

3. From morning until night, the little red bird worked very hard. She had a lot of jobs to do that day. She asked her children for help. But they wanted to play. She asked her friends, but they were too busy. She asked her neighbors for help, but they were also too busy. No other bird helped her at all. She got food from the garden. She made some bread, too. The food smelled very good. Then her children, friends, and neighbors came to help her. They wanted to help her to eat the food. The little red bird said, "No."

   a. Is this story a fable? _____

   b. Does it teach a lesson? _____

   c. What is the moral of this story? _____

   _____

4. A little duck was swimming in the water. She looked around, and she saw a big black bear. The bear was hungry, and it was looking for food. This bear really liked to eat little ducks. The duck was afraid. So she quickly put her head under the water. She couldn't see the bear anymore. But the bear could see her.

   a. Is this story a fable? _____

   b. Does it teach a lesson? _____

   c. What is the moral of this story? _____

   _____

 ## Let's Find Out About You!

You have read several fables. Which one do you like the best? Does it have a special meaning to you? Why? Do you like to learn from fables? Which lesson is most important for you to learn?

Step 8

Before You Read

1. What do you do for a headache?
2. What medicines do you have at home?
3. Why do people go to doctors?

Always Read the Label

1   A sick person usually goes to a doctor, because a doctor can help. The doctor checks the person for signs of sickness and asks her questions. What are some doctor's questions?

"What's the problem?"

5   "How do you feel?"

"Where does it hurt?"

"What did you eat?"

What does a doctor do? She checks the patient. She looks at her carefully. The doctor checks the sick person's

10   mouth. She looks at her tongue. She checks the person's eyes, ears, nose, and throat. Then she takes the patient's temperature. She puts her hand on the person's face. Does her face feel hot? Is her face red? Of course, the doctor also uses a thermometer. The thermometer shows the patient's

15   temperature. What is her temperature? Is it normal?

Ninety-eight point six degrees Fahrenheit (98.6°F) is normal temperature. Thirty-seven degrees Celsius (37°C) is normal too. In other words, 37 degrees Celsius equals 98.6 degrees Fahrenheit. A temperature above normal is

20   called a fever. Does the person have a fever? A fever is a sign of sickness in a patient.

A doctor understands sickness. She also knows about medicines for sicknesses. She writes a special note for the sick person. It is a note to a pharmacist, or a prescription.

25   It is a prescription for medicine.

The doctor says to the patient, "Take this prescription to the drugstore. Give it to the pharmacist. The pharmacist will fill the prescription. He or she will give you pills. The pills are your medicine."

30   The doctor also says, "Read the label. Read it carefully. Labels are important."

The sick person goes to the drugstore. She gives the prescription to the pharmacist. The pharmacist follows the doctor's orders and fills the prescription. Then the

35   pharmacist puts a label on the bottle and gives the pills to the sick person. The pharmacist explains the medicine to the sick person. It is the pharmacist's job to explain how to use the medicine. Then what does the pharmacist say? He or she says, "READ THE LABEL!"

40   What is a label? It is the note on a medicine bottle. It gives information. For example, it tells the times to take the medicine. It says, "Take one pill twice a day." What does this label mean? It means: Take two pills every day. Take one in the morning. Take one at night.

45   Some medicines can be dangerous. Every sick person must read the medicine label. He or she must read it carefully. The person must also follow the directions on the label. The directions are very important.

A doctor knows best. A patient must always follow

50   the doctor's advice. The doctor's directions help stop the sickness. Medicines can make a person feel well again.

≈| Let's Learn from the Reading!

1. Who does a patient go to see? _____

2. What does a thermometer do?
   a. It tells a person's temperature.
   b. It gives pills to a sick person.
   c. It gives directions.
   d. It writes a prescription.

3. What is the main idea of "Always Read the Label"?

    a. Doctors can help their patients.

    b. The label on a medicine bottle is important.

    c. A pharmacist knows about medicines.

    d. Many pills are dangerous.

4. What did you learn from "Always Read the Label"?

    a. Thirty-seven degrees Celsius is not a normal temperature.

    b. A prescription is the same as a label on a bottle of medicine.

    c. It is the pharmacist's job to explain how to use the medicine.

    d. Doctors go to drugstores to buy medicines for sick people.

5. Which sentence is in "Always Read the Label"? Find the sentence in the reading and underline it.

    a. The note for medicine is a prescription.

    b. The doctor checks the sick person's mouth.

    c. Sick people go to a drugstore to see a doctor.

    d. A prescription is the note on a pill bottle.

6. What is a label? _____

7. What is on a pill bottle? _____

8. What is on a medicine label? _____

9. What is a normal temperature in Celsius and in Fahrenheit?

    _____   _____

10. Who writes a prescription? _____

11. Who fills a prescription? Who sells the medicine to a sick person?

    _____

12. Who needs a prescription? _____

Let's Practice!

A. *True* or *False?*

Write *true* or *false* in each blank.

1. _____ A label on a bottle of medicine has important information about the medicine.

2. _____ Pills are a kind of medicine.

3. _____ Doctors usually work in drugstores.

4. _____ A prescription from a doctor gives directions to a pharmacist.

5. _____ A doctor checks a sick man for signs of sickness.

6. _____ Medicine bottles usually do not have labels.

7. _____ A pharmacist works with a doctor to help a sick person.

8. _____ It is important to follow the directions on medicine bottles.

9. _____ There is nothing dangerous in medicines.

10. _____ A thermometer is like a prescription.

11. _____ One sign of sickness is a fever.

12. _____ A patient is a person who goes to see a doctor.

13. _____ A doctor's advice is like directions to a sick person.

14. _____ A normal temperature is a fever.

15. _____ It is a pharmacist's job to take a sick person's temperature to check for fever.

B. Find the Different Word

One word is different from the others. Which word is different? How are the others alike? Can you say? Draw a circle around the different word.

1.   pharmacist   medicine   patient   doctor

2.   look at   check   hurt

3.   Fahrenheit   Celsius   degree

4.	directions	medicine	pills	
5.	thermometer	temperature	pharmacist	
6.	normal	sick	pill	
7.	throat	mouth	nose	note
8.	directions	advice	fever	label
9.	prescription	drugstore	label	note
10.	doctor	feel	open	say

C. Drugstores

All over the world, drugstores are the places for getting medicines. Some drugstores also have other things for sale. For example, some drugstores sell food. Many sell newspapers, books, and magazines too.

Many drugstores sell make-up, also. *Make-up* is another word for *cosmetics*. Cosmetics are things like lipstick and face powder. Drugstores also sell important things for everyone. For example, many people want to buy shampoo and soap. So, drugstores have shampoo and soap for them to buy. In fact, drugstores carry many things that people need in a hurry. Therefore, drugstores in many neighborhoods often carry milk!

Draw a circle around all the things from a drugstore.

thermometers	shampoo	stamps	drinks	milk
prescriptions	cigarettes	houses	books	soap
blackboards	medicine	pencils	chairs	pens
newspapers	pictures	bottles	tables	beds
magazines	flowers	apples	paper	pills
ice cream	powder	clocks	cards	cars
calendars	lipstick	candy	food	

Let's Talk!

Read the two questions carefully. Plan your answer. Then tell your answers to another person in the class. Do you have some of the same answers?

1. You go to drugstores, don't you? What do you usually buy at the drugstore?

2. Most medicine bottles have special tops. Their covers do not come off easily. There is a good reason for this. Do you know the reason? What is it?

Let's Write!

Here are two writing ideas for you and your classmates.

1. A Special Label

   All medicines have one special label. It says:

   KEEP OUT OF THE REACH OF CHILDREN!

   What does this label mean?

   _____

   _____

2. Here are some more labels. What do these labels mean?

   a. Take once a day as directed.

   _____

   b. Take one for pain.

   _____

   c. Take two or three pills after meals when needed.

   _____

   d. Take one pill half an hour before each meal.

   _____

e. Take with water only, as directed.

_____

f. Do not take with milk.

_____

g. Take with food.

_____

 Let's Write More!

A doctor asks a sick person many questions: Where does it hurt? What is sore? How do you feel? Do you have a headache?

Here are some words for parts of the body. Any part of the body can *hurt*. We use the word *ache* for some parts of the body. That is, some parts of the body have aches and other parts of the body are sore, but usually not both—except for the back. A patient can have a sore back or a backache, and his or her back hurts.

Look at each picture and write a sentence for the person.

Head
"My head hurts."
"I have a headache."

_____

_____

_____

Throat
"My throat hurts."
"I have a sore throat."

_____

_____

_____

Tooth
"My tooth hurts."
"I have a toothache."

_____

_____

_____

Ear
"My ear hurts."
"I have an earache."

_____

_____

_____

Eye
"My eye hurts."
"I have a sore eye."

_____

_____

_____

Foot
"My foot hurts."
"I have a sore foot."

_____

_____

_____

Hand
"My hand hurts."
"I have a sore hand."

_____

_____

_____

Stomach
"My stomach hurts."
"I have a stomachache."

_____

_____

_____

Back
"My back hurts."
"I have a sore back."
"I have a backache."

_____

_____

_____

 Let's Find Out About You!

How do you feel right now? Does any part of you feel sore? Does any part of you ache? Do you need any medicine every day? How does medicine help you?

Step 9

Before You Read

1. How do people help one another?
   (Think of many different ways.)

2. Here is a proverb: "Two heads are better than one."
   What does it mean?

3. Here is another famous line: "No man is an island."
   What does this line mean?

A Tradition of Cooperation

1   The tradition of cooperation is as old as history. People have always helped one another. In the early days of the Old West in North America, neighbors needed their neighbors. Life was difficult. People lived on farms away from other families. They went to town once a week or one time a month. Then they saw their friends and neighbors. On their farms everyone had lots of work. There were many jobs to do. And there were some big problems. How did one family make a house? How could they build a barn alone? Those were big jobs. They needed to help one another. Cooperation became a tradition.

It is not easy for one family to build a house or a barn alone. So these families asked for help. They asked their friends and neighbors. First the family prepared everything for the building. They got the wood ready, and they prepared the place for the building. Then they invited other people to a work party for a few days. The women worked together, took care of the children together, and cooked together. They made breakfast, lunch, and dinner. The men worked on the building.

For the children it was like a holiday. There were many other children to play with. They enjoyed it very much. They played games together, and they helped with the work too.

Together these people built a house or a barn. At another time the family with the new house would help neighbors. They all helped one another with big jobs. The people worked together for the good of everyone.

A work party is really cooperation. *To cooperate* means
30 "to work together." A big job can be easy if many people
work together. Then the big job becomes a small job for
many workers. Working together can be fun, too.

The tradition of cooperation is changing. Today there
isn't so much cooperation. People don't work together
35 very much. Some people don't even know their neighbors'
names. How can they ask them for help?

Today, the idea of cooperation is unusual. We often
work against cooperation. We work alone, not with others.
It is normal for us to build fences by ourselves.

40 Today, we wait for emergencies. We wait for accidents
to happen. After an emergency or an accident, we are
willing to help. Then we want to help. Then we talk to our
neighbors. Then we become true neighbors and friends.

Why don't we always cooperate? Why do we wait for
45 emergencies or accidents? Why don't we work with other
people? It can be fun. Life can become easier, too.

Let's from the Reading!

1. What were the early days like in the Old West?
   a. People worked very hard because life was difficult.
   b. People built fences to keep others away.
   c. People had a lot of fun because they lived near their neighbors.
   d. People lived in big houses on farms in large groups.

2. What is the main idea of "A Tradition of Cooperation"?
   a. People ask their neighbors for help.
   b. A family can make a big house.
   c. People build fences and not barns.
   d. Working together means easier work and fun for everyone.

3. In the days of the Old West, people cooperated with one another. Now people don't work together very often. What does this mean?

   a. People don't ask for help.

   b. People don't know their neighbors.

   c. Cooperation isn't fun anymore.

   d. Life is easier with cooperation.

4. Which sentence is in "A Tradition of Cooperation"? Find the sentence in the reading and underline it.

   a. Today there is a lot of cooperation.

   b. A big job can be easy if many people work together.

   c. The people worked together to help their neighbors.

   d. The people worked together for the good of everyone.

5. In the early days of the Old West, how did a family build a house?

   _____

   _____

6. How can a big job become easy?

   _____

7. An accident is…

   a. an emergency.

   b. an idea.

   c. cooperation.

   d. fun at work.

Let's Practice!

A. *True* or *False?*

Write *true* or *false* in each blank.

1. _____ A family needs a home.

2. _____ History is the story of people who live in one place together.

3. _____ Cooperating makes big jobs easier.

4. _____ Fences are like houses.

5. _____ Neighbors can help to make a house.

6. _____ An accident is a kind of emergency.

7. _____ Most people are willing to help others in an emergency.

8. _____ A farm doesn't really need a barn.

B. Find the Different Word or Phrase

In each group, there is one different word or phrase. It belongs to a different group of words. Can you find the different word? Draw a circle around the different one. What makes the other words a group?

1.	hard	difficult	problem	not easy
2.	work	problem	job	
3.	fence	house	barn	
4.	make	help	build	
5.	came	built	help	became
6.	willing	accident	emergency	
7.	job	cooperation	working together	
8.	family	neighbors	friends	ourselves
9.	true	fun	play	
10.	food	lunch	breakfast	dinner

◆ | **Let's Read More!**

More About Cooperation

1   Cooperation was important to early farmers in the Old West. They worked together, and they did big jobs. They did not have big machines. There were no tractors. They did not have many tools either. What did they have? They had
5   only themselves and their neighbors. They had good will—and the willingness to cooperate. They had a tradition of helping.

Working together was a way of life. The men worked in the fields together. They planted crops together. They
10   gathered the crops together.

The women helped one another also. They helped one another with food. They had "bees." A bee is a work party. Everyone came to a bee. Together, they did big jobs easily. They even worked together to make quilts. A quilt
15   is a blanket for a bed. The women saved bits of cloth. Then they used the small pieces of cloth to make quilts. One woman alone worked a long time to make a quilt. The work was slow. Together, the women did the job fast. They made a quilt in only one day. They also talked together
20   and helped one another with problems. They learned from one another too.

Farmers cooperate even today. There are "farmers' cooperatives." These organizations are like big clubs, but they are work clubs. The cooperative or "co-op" is a group
25   of farmers. The co-op works for the farmers. It sells the farmers' crops, and it buys necessary things for the farmers. The co-op buys big farm machines. It buys tractors and farm tools. The farmers all use these machines and tools.

The cooperative sometimes has a store. The farmers can
30   buy necessary things at their co-op.

Members of the cooperative work at their store. They
can save money this way. They get to know their neighbors
too. A cooperative organization helps all the people in it.

≈ | Let's Learn from the Reading!

1. What happens at a quilting bee?

   _____

   _____

2. What is a work club?

   _____

   _____

3. What is a farmers' cooperative? How does it work?

   _____

   _____

4. What is any kind of "bee"? (Circle all the right answers.)
   a. A bee is big work party.
   b. A bee is cooperating to do a big job.
   c. A bee is a neighbor.
   d. A bee is a big job.

5. What is a "member" of a cooperative? (Circle all the right answers.)
   a. a person
   b. a doctor or a pharmacist
   c. usually a part of a family that has a farm
   d. someone who became part of the organization
   e. a neighbor
   f. a child

Let's Practice!

A. Find the Same Meaning

Draw a line between the two words or phrases with similar meanings.

1. people who live nearby	a. plant or gather crops
2. a bed blanket	b. a work party
3. work in the fields	c. cooperate
4. too	d. lunch
5. pieces	e. an emergency
6. food at noon (12:00)	f. bits
7. a farm machine	g. a barn
8. history	h. tractor
9. an accident	i. neighbors
10. a bee	j. a quilt
11. a place for animals	k. also
12. work together	l. the story of a group of people

B. Find the Right Word or Phrase

Fill in the blanks to finish the sentences.

A cooperative store is a " _____ ." Members of the cooperative work at this store. They buy necessary things for their _____ . They buy _____ and _____ _____ . They buy from their own store. In this way, they can _____ money. At the cooperative store, farmers _____ to _____ their neighbors too.

Let's Talk!

Ask a friend in the class these questions. Then answer them yourself. Talk about your answers.

1. Is there a cooperative near your home? What is the name of the cooperative?

2. Are you a member of a cooperative store? Could you become a member?

3. Do your neighbors cooperate much? How could you cooperate more with them?

4. Do you like to work with others? Why is it fun to work with others?

 Let's Write!

A. Here are some ideas for cooperation. What will the people do?

1. Make lunch for twenty-five people.

   What will you have to eat?

   What will the people do?

   Person A will _____ .

   Person B will _____ .

   Person C will _____ .

   Person D will _____ .

2. An old woman needs help with her house. It needs cleaning. You and four friends want to help. What will each of you do?

a. The glass in all the windows is dirty.

   I will _____wash_____ it.

b. The kitchen is dirty.

   My friend _____ .

c. The floor is dirty.

   My friend _____ .

d. _____ is dirty.

    My friend _____ .

e. _____ is dirty.

    My friend _____ .

B. "Make a Difference Day"

Do you know about "Make a Difference Day"? Every year, on the same day, people work together to fix something or clean something. They make important changes. What work can you and your classmates do on Make a Difference Day? Answer these questions on a piece of paper, and make a short paragraph.

1. What job can you do?

2. What tools do you need to do the job?

3. How long will the job take you?

4. What difference can you make?

5. What will the result of your work be?

6. Who will you help?

Let's Find Out About You!

Are you good at cooperation? You and your classmates can make a cooperative. All of you need paper and pencils, for example. You can buy one box of paper and use it together. It will cost less in a big box. Make a list of other necessary items. How much does each one cost now?

_____   _____

_____   _____

_____   _____

1. We need _____ .

    Now each one costs _____ .

    We can buy a box for $ _____ .

    Then each one will cost _____ .

2. We need _____ .

    Now each one costs _____ .

    We can buy a box for $ _____ .

    Then each one will cost _____ .

3. We need _____ .

    Now each one costs _____ .

    We can buy a box for $ _____ .

    Then each one will cost _____ .

4. We need _____ .

    Now each one costs _____ .

    We can buy a box for $ _____ .

    Then each one will cost _____ .

5. We need _____ .

   Now each one costs _____ .

   We can buy a box for $ _____ .

   Then each one will cost _____ .

Now ask yourself these questions:

1. Did I enjoy cooperating?
2. Do people save money by cooperating?
3. Will you join in other cooperative work?

Step 10

Before You Read

1. What makes a city really beautiful?
2. What makes a city look bad?
3. What can people do to keep cities beautiful?

Keep It Clean!

1   Many of the big cities of the world have a serious problem. The air is dirty, and the water is dirty. Even the streets are dirty. Some pollution comes from factories. Factories make a lot of smoke, and the smoke makes the

5   air bad. Cars do the same thing. They add bad things to the air. It is not healthy for people to breathe that air. Polluted air can make people very sick.

    Some of the pollution comes from people who don't care. People usually have clean houses, don't they? They

10   usually have clean yards, too. But their streets are not clean. You can see it for yourself. Just walk down the street. Look down at the ground. What do you see? You see paper, and you see cigarette ends. You see broken bottles and newspapers. Look in lakes and rivers, and you will

15   see garbage there, too. What a shame! The people who live there have health problems because of the pollution. In fact, it is a very serious problem. The problem is not easy to understand either.

    To see an example, go to a park. Of course, some parks

20   are clean, but some are very dirty. In a dirty park, what do you see? There is litter everywhere.

    Some children throw paper from candy on the ground. People throw away soft-drink cans. There are broken bottles and newspapers too. Where does all the garbage come from?

25   Some families have picnics. That is easy to understand because parks are for picnics. There are tables for picnics, and there are garbage cans. People sit at the tables to eat. But some people don't use the garbage cans. Many people go home and leave their garbage at the park. Some people

30 leave food. Some leave paper plates. They leave empty bags and garbage everywhere. Is their park clean? Is it clean for other people?

Other families come to the park. They see the litter. They think, "The park is already dirty, so we can throw
35 litter on the ground too. We can leave our garbage here. It doesn't matter." People like them don't care about the park.

Go to the beach. Do people care about it? Is the sand clean? Probably not. Is the water clean? It probably isn't either. There is garbage in the water, so the water isn't
40 clean anymore.

Don't people keep their homes clean? Don't people keep their own yards clean? Then why aren't the streets clean? Why aren't the parks and the beaches clean? This problem is hard to understand.

45 There are some cities that are not dirty. They do not have this problem of pollution. They have clean streets. Their parks are clean like their yards. There are not many cars on the streets. The factories are clean too. People in these cities work together. They cooperate for a clean city.
50 These people care about their city, their air, and their water.

Let's Learn from the Reading!

1. What are two reasons for air pollution? _____

   and _____

2. What is litter?
   a. Litter is picnic food.
   b. Litter is garbage on the ground.
   c. Litter is dirty ground.
   d. Litter is the park.

3. What is the main idea of "Keep It Clean!"?
   a. Parks are for picnics and fun.
   b. Some people do not care about keeping their cities clean.
   c. The streets of all cities are dirty.
   d. People throw away soft-drink cans.

4. Some people have clean homes and clean yards. But their parks and streets are dirty. What does this mean?
   a. There are no garbage cans in the streets.
   b. Many people don't go home. They go to the parks.
   c. Some people care about their homes, but not about their parks.
   d. Some people cooperate with others for a clean city.

5. Which sentence is in "Keep It Clean"? Find the sentence in the reading and underline it.
   a. Don't people keep their houses clean?
   b. Other cities do not have this problem.
   c. They don't use the garbage cans.
   d. People like them don't care about the park.

6. Where is there sand? It is...
   a. in the park.
   b. on the beach.
   c. in the garbage can.
   d. in the yard.

7. Who uses paper plates?

   a. dirty children

   b. garbage cans

   c. families at picnics

   d. people in clean cities

8. What does *cooperate* mean? _____

9. What is a picnic?

   a. People throw litter on the ground.

   b. People leave paper plates at the park.

   c. People eat together outdoors.

   d. People eat together at home.

10. What kinds of garbage do you see on the streets?

   _____

11. Why is the water in lakes and rivers dirty?

   _____

12. Which of these things go into a garbage can? (Circle all the right
    answers.)

   a. paper plates   i. cars

   b. cigarette ends   j. sand

   c. smoke   k. tables

   d. food   l. soft-drink cans

   e. children   m. paper

   f. empty bags   n. newspapers

   g. broken bottles   o. books

   h. garbage

◆ **Let's Read More!**

What Can We Do About Litter?

1   What can a city do about litter? Garbage on the streets is a big problem. There are some answers to this problem. A city can buy more garbage cans. But usually that doesn't help much. In some cities, people don't use garbage cans.

5   The police can help. They can watch for litterbugs. Litterbugs are people who throw garbage on the ground. The police can tell them to stop! But sometimes even the police cannot help much. Some people don't care. They still throw garbage on the ground.

10   All people must want to keep parks and streets clean. Advertising can help! People can talk about the problem on the radio and television. They can ask for help. You can ask for help. You can ask your neighbors to care about the city.

        Here is a popular saying: "Every little bit counts." In a

15 city, every little bit of litter makes a difference. Every little bit of garbage makes a city dirty. Every "litter" bit of garbage in a garbage can helps to make a clean city.

        People can make a city clean or dirty. In fact, only people can make the difference between clean and dirty.

◎ **Let's Practice!**

A. *True* or *False*?

Write *true* or *false* in each blank.

1. _____   There are broken bottles in parks and even in rivers.

2. _____   Smoke is a reason for air pollution.

3. _____   People throw garbage in their yards.

4. _____ A park is all around a house.

5. _____ Sand at a beach is usually clean.

6. _____ *Cooperate* means work together.

7. _____ People usually use paper plates for picnics.

8. _____ Parks are for people to enjoy.

9. _____ More cars means dirtier air in a city.

10. _____ Some people don't care about parks.

11. _____ You can buy soft drinks in a can.

12. _____ A lot of candy has paper around it.

B. Find the Different Word

One word in each group doesn't belong there. It is different from the other words. Can you find the different word? How is it different from the others? How are the other words alike? Draw a circle around the different word.

1.	clean	dirty	garbage	
2.	yard	house	park	
3.	city	people	family	
4.	see	say	look	
5.	leave	keep	dirty	
6.	candy	soft drink	bottle	
7.	soft drink	can	water	
8.	dirty	hard	easy	
9.	matter	litter	garbage	
10.	can	bottle	paper	plate
11.	food	garbage	litter	pollution
12.	picnic	lunch	bottles	breakfast
13.	park	yard	beach	water

C. Find the Same Meaning

Draw a line between the two words or phrases with similar meanings.

1. I don't care   a. beach

2. litter   b. picnic

3. smoke   c. cooperate

4. work together   d. dirty

5. not clean   e. it doesn't matter

6. lunch in the park or at the beach   f. pollution

7. sand near the water   g. important and dangerous

8. serious   h. garbage

D. Let's Have a Picnic!

Let's talk about a picnic. Fill in the blanks with new words.

1. Let's have a _____ on the sandy beach.

2. There are some big _____ for us to sit at and eat.

3. We can take _____ to eat.

4. Let's buy _____ _____ to put the food on.

5. Let's buy soft drinks in _____ or bottles.

6. We will have a lot of fun.

7. We will take _____ home with us from the beach.

8. We will not throw _____ on the sand or in the water.

9. We will put the garbage in a big _____ _____ .

10. Then the beach will be clean.

Let's Talk!

A. Find the names of these things.

1. What are the names of some soft drinks?

2. What are the names of some picnic foods?

3. What are some things to buy in bottles?

4. What are some things to buy with paper all around them?

B. Some parks have a sign: "No glass bottles!"

What do you think of that idea? Why is it a good idea?

 Let's Write!

What does a clean city have? Read the list of ideas here. Choose some ideas to write a paragraph about a clean city. There are some ideas to help you write a paragraph. But be careful! Some of the ideas in the list are not right! Be careful of these wrong ideas! Perhaps you can make all the ideas right. Then write about cities in the space on page 135.

_____	busy streets	_____	tall buildings
_____	clean sidewalks	_____	lots of trees
_____	garbage cans for litter	_____	open spaces
_____	parks with tables	_____	museums
_____	lots of trees	_____	libraries
_____	nice barns	_____	large schools
_____	pretty gardens	_____	lots of cars
_____	big fields	_____	factories
_____	nice houses	_____	wide roads and streets
_____	clean lakes and rivers	_____	theaters
_____	beautiful beaches	_____	places to buy things

What Do Cities Have?

Cities can be nice places to live. There are many reasons that people like to live in cities. For example, _____

_____

_____

_____

_____

    Some things about cities are very important to me. I like to live in a city with _____

_____

_____

_____

_____

    Cities are full of people. That is why it is easy for a city to get dirty. However, if people work together, they can keep it clean. A clean city is beautiful for many reasons. First of all, a clean city has

_____

_____

_____

_____

Let's Practice More!

Here are three exercises. Your teacher will ask you to do one, two, or all of them.

1. What can you find in a garbage can? What do people throw away? Make a list of five things:

   a. _old newspapers_

   b. _____

   c. _____

   d. _____

   e. _____

2. If you want to go on a picnic, what food will you buy? Make a list of foods and non-foods.

   a. _something to drink_

   b. _____

   c. _____

   d. _____

   e. _____

3. The opposite of *clean* is *dirty*. *Dirty* means *not clean*. Do you know other word pairs like clean and dirty? Make a list of opposites. Use the words in this list:

   a. cold _____

   b. question _____

   c. begin _____

   d. healthy _____

   e. big _____

   f. old _____

g. yes _____

h. small _____

i. tall _____

j. many _____

k. healthy _____

l. right _____

m. dangerous _____

n. expensive _____

Do you know some other pairs of opposites? Write them here:

_____   _____

_____   _____

_____   _____

 Let's Find Out About You!

What are your ideas about pollution? Do you think pollution is dangerous? Do you think it is bad to leave garbage on the ground? Why or why not?

Plateau II
What We Wear

Before You Read

With your classmates, talk about these questions. Your teacher or a classmate will write new words on the board.

1. Why are clothes important to all people? Why are they important to you?
2. Is fashion important to you?
3. How much do clothes cost?
4. Do all clothes cost a lot of money?
5. Can a person get clothes and not spend a lot of money? How? Where?
6. Do nice clothes make a difference? How?
7. What do you think about this saying? "Clothes make the man." Is it true?
8. Do clothes "make" a woman? If so, how does what a person wears make a difference?

The History of Clothing

1   In the first days of human history, people lived in caves, not houses. Historians today call them "cave people." Cave people did not wear many clothes. In the summer, they did not need clothes at all because the weather was not

5   cold. In hot weather, clothes for them were not important. In the winter, the temperature fell. The people were cold, so they needed something to keep warm. They wore animal skins. Today, we still use animal skins for some of our clothing. We use animal skins to make leather, and we wear

10   leather clothes. Fur coats come from animal skins too.

Today we make clothes from other natural materials, too. Wool comes from sheep. The fibers, or long pieces of wool, become thread. The thread becomes wool cloth. Wool makes a warm cloth. It is good for winter clothes.

15   People have used wool for clothing for many many years.

Summer clothes are usually cotton. Cotton material comes from a plant. The plant has long white fibers. The cotton fibers make a light cloth. Cotton makes the coolest clothing. However, cotton grows only where the summer

20   weather is very hot. So cotton was not common around the world.

Cotton and wool are natural fibers. There are two more kinds of cloth from natural fibers. They are silk and linen. Little worms (silkworms) make silk fibers. However,

25   silkworms eat only the leaves of one kind of tree, the mulberry tree. This tree does not grow in every climate. Also, silk cloth is not easy to make. Silk is expensive for

30 these two reasons. Linen is difficult to make too. It comes from a plant that is called flax. Linen is also expensive because it is difficult to make. However, flax grows in places with cool climates, so it was common. To make cloth for warm weather, people mixed the fibers of wool

35 and flax. This cloth was more comfortable for summer clothing. (They called it "linsey-woolsey.")

Cotton, wool, silk, and flax—all these fibers become thread. The name for thread-making is spinning. Thread becomes cloth. Many people have to work together to make

40 cloth. Many people work to make clothes, too. A spinner makes the thread. A weaver makes the cloth. Then someone makes the cloth into clothes. A seamstress is a woman who makes clothes. A tailor also makes clothes, but tailors are usually men.

45 Many years ago, families made their own clothes. Sewing was an important job in every home.

≋| Let's Learn from the Reading!

1. Why didn't cave people wear clothing in the summer?
    a. They wore linen clothes. It was not cold then.
    b. They didn't need to wear clothes. The weather was warm.
    c. They wore wool clothes. It was warm in the summer.
    d. They wore fur and leather because they lived in cold caves.

2. How do we use animal skins for clothes today?

    _____

    _____

3. What are some natural fibers?

   _____

   _____

4. What do we get wool from?

   _____

5. Why is silk expensive? It is expensive because…
   a. it is difficult to make.
   b. little silkworms don't like to work.
   c. it is a natural fiber.
   d. plants don't make fibers in the winter.

6. Which natural fibers come from plants?
   a. wool
   b. cotton
   c. linen
   d. silk

7. Which natural fibers come from animals?
   a. wool
   b. cotton
   c. linen
   d. silk

8. Why is wool good for winter clothes?

   _____

9. What is the name for thread-making?

   _____

10. What is the difference between a tailor and a seamstress?

   _____

Let's Practice!

A. Complete the Sentences

Fill in the blanks with these words.

spinning	weaver	fibers	leather	wool
mulberry	worms	tailor	cotton	flax

1. A _____ makes cloth.

2. Silk, linen, cotton, and wool are all natural _____ .

3. Linen comes from a plant called _____ .

4. A person makes thread by _____ .

5. _____ makes warm clothes.

6. Today, we make _____ out of animal skins.

7. A _____ makes clothes.

8. Use _____ cloth to make cool clothes for warm weather.

9. Little _____ make silk fibers.

10. These little worms eat only the leaves from _____ trees.

B. Using Question Words

Here are some questions and short answers. Fill in the blanks.

Who/What makes what?

1. What makes wool?   A _____ does.

2. Who makes thread?   A _____ does.

3. Who makes cloth?   A _____ does.

4. Who makes clothes?   A _____ or a _____ does.

5. What makes silk?   _____ do.

6. Who used animal skins for clothing?   _____ did.

Let's Read More!

Buying Clothes

1   Today, most people do not make their own clothes. They go to a store to look for good clothes and buy them. They find nice colors and beautiful styles.

Asperson can try on clothes at a store. Does the dress
5   fit? Are the pants long enough? Does the color look good? Is the style right for the person? A person can go to the store and find out. A person tries on clothes. Some clothes look nice and sell for a good price. People buy these clothes.

Store clothes are called ready-made or ready-to-wear.
10   They come in many sizes. There are sizes for babies. There are sizes for children, too. Teenagers have special sizes. So do men and women. Clothing sizes follow body measurements. How does a person know her size? She uses a tape measure. She measures her chest and her waist. Hips
15   and height are important too. Then she looks on a size chart for measurements like hers. Then she knows her size.

≃ **Let's Learn from the Reading!**

1. What are ready-to-wear clothes? _____

2. Why do people try clothes on? They try on clothes…
   a. to measure them.   c. to look at the price.
   b. to look at a size chart.   d. to find the right size.

3. How can a person find out his size? _____

4. What does a chart show? _____

5. What do people use to measure themselves for clothing?

_____

@ | **Let's Practice!**

Look at this chart for boys' sizes. It shows measurements and sizes.

Note: 12 inches = 1 foot
        1 inch = 2.5 centimeters
        10 centimeters = 4 inches

Measurement Chart

BOYS' SIZES

Order Size	Height Inches	Average Chest Inches	Average Waist Inches	Husky Chest Inches	Husky Waist Inches
8 or 8H	49-52	26-27	23-24	29-30	26-27
10 or 10H	53-55	27-28	24-25	30-31	27-28
12 or 12H	56-59	29-30	25-26	32-33	28-29
14 or 14H	60-62	30-32	26-27	33-35	29-30

What sizes do these boys need?

1. Robby Bellows is 54 inches tall. His chest measurement is 28 inches. His waist is 25 inches. What is his size? _____

2. Robby's older brother is five feet tall. His chest is 33 inches. His waist is 29 inches. What size does he need? _____

3. Robby's younger brother is 48 inches tall. His chest is 30 inches, and his waist is 26 inches. What size does he wear? _____

 ## Let's Read More!

Big Sale

1   Everyone waits for sales. They look in newspapers because they advertise sales. Good shoppers look for sales because at a sale, prices are low. A good shopper can save money at a sale.

5   Sales can also be bad for shoppers because sometimes shoppers buy unnecessary things. They spend money, and they don't save money. They buy without a plan for using the things that they buy.

    Stores have sales for several reasons. At the end of
10   summer, cool clothing goes on sale because people want to buy warm winter clothes. The store cannot keep summer clothing, too. So, the store sells summer clothes cheap. Good shoppers buy their summer clothes at the end of summer. They buy clothing in larger sizes for their children
15   for the next year. That is why fall is a good time to buy summer clothes.

    There is another reason for sales. For example, a store sells a popular item for a very low price. Shoppers come to buy this one item, but they buy other things, too. This
20   kind of sale is very popular. But a good shopper is always careful. At a sale like this, prices for other items are often higher. A careful shopper buys only sale items.

    Stores also have sales for out-of-fashion clothes. Fashions in clothing, especially clothing for teenagers,
25   change very fast. A careful shopper understands this fact and does not buy these clothes. Teenagers do not like to wear clothes that are out of style. In fact, they won't wear clothing that isn't in fashion!

At a store, you pay for the clothes and get a receipt.
30   Keep this little piece of paper. It shows payment for the clothes. If you have to take something back to the store, you will need the receipt.

There is one important thing to remember about sales. Ask yourself this question before buying anything: What
35   do I really need?

___

Let's Learn from the Reading!

1. When is a good time to buy winter clothing?

2. Why do stores have sales? Stores have sales because…

    a. good shoppers buy clothes at sales.

    b. stores sell summer clothes cheaper.

    c. stores need a place for new clothes.

    d. people want to buy winter clothes in the fall.

3. What kind of clothes does a good shopper not buy on sale?

    _____

4. What is a teenager? _____

5. What shows payment for something in a store?

    a. money

    b. clothes

    c. receipt

    d. piece

Let's Read More!

What Do You Really Need?

1   Are you a careful shopper? A good shopper always goes to a sale with a plan. Do you make a list of necessary clothes items? What do you really need? What does your family need? In a notebook, write down the needed
5   clothing. Write down the sizes and measurements of the people in your family. Keep this notebook with you on a shopping trip. Take it to every sale.

    At the store, look for good quality. Well-made clothes are good for many years. Poor (or bad) quality is a waste of
10 money. Also choose colors carefully. Do not buy unusual colors. Plan to mix and match your clothes. Then you will have many combinations of clothes to wear.

 Let's Learn from the Reading!

1. A shopping plan is a good idea because…
    a. you need to make many combinations of clothes.
    b. your notes will help you to buy only necessary things.
    c. you want to mix and match the sizes.
    d. advertising is always difficult to understand.

2. Mix-and-match clothes are…
    a. clothes that you can wear in different combinations.
    b. clothes with unusual colors.
    c. clothing that you really need.
    d. good-quality items in unusual colors and styles.

3. Why are mix-and-match items good to buy? They are good buys because...

   a. you can find them at every sale.

   b. you can wear them with unusual colors.

   c. you can try them on at the store.

   d. you can wear them with many different clothes.

4. Why is good quality in clothes important?

_____

5. What information does a good shopper write in a shopping notebook?

_____

6. Why are unusual colors not a good buy? They are not good to buy because...

   a. they are not on your list of necessary items.

   b. they are difficult to mix and match.

   c. you can make unusual combinations with them.

   d. they are always in fashion.

 Let's Read More!

Ways to Save Money on Clothing

1   If you want to save on clothes, buy only necessary clothes. Check your closet. What colors do you have? What colors mix and match with your clothes? What colors are good on you? What basic styles do you wear? What styles
5   are the most comfortable for you to wear? What kind of clothing do you need? Do you need business clothing or sports clothing? How many formal clothes do you need? Clothes should fit your lifestyle.

Before a shopping trip, make a shopping list. Go to
10   several stores. Compare the prices and the quality.

What kind of clothes costs the most? Formal clothing
is usually very expensive, and people do not wear formal
clothes very often. Perhaps you need something formal
to wear. Try to find a less formal dress or suit. Then you
15   can wear it more often. It is better to buy a skirt and a
sweater than to buy a dress, for example. It is better to
buy a jacket and pants than a suit. Then you can wear the
sweater and the jacket with different things. Clothes of
basic solid colors go with many things. For example,
20   women will understand that a black skirt, a red sweater, a
dark jacket, and a white shirt are easy to mix and match
with other clothes. For a man, dark pants, a white shirt or
a blue shirt, and a navy blue (dark blue) jacket (a blazer)
are a good combination.

25   Look in different departments. Women can wear men's
sweaters and T-shirts. These items are often cheaper than
women's clothes.

Some discount stores have good clothing at low prices.
Try second-hand stores, too. These stores sell used clothes.
30   Another place to go is a surplus store. Second-hand stores
and surplus stores do not have expensive decorations.
They can sell clothing cheaper. But check the clothing
carefully. Look for quality.

Many stores often have sales. Watch for these sales, but
35   be sure to buy only needed items.

Let's Learn from the Reading!

1. Which stores have lower prices on clothes?

   _____

2. It is a good idea to go to several stores and compare prices before buying because...

   a. some stores do not have expensive decorations.

   b. women can wear men's clothes.

   c. many stores often sell used clothes.

   d. you can find good prices and save money.

3. Why are discount, surplus, and second-hand stores cheaper?

   _____

4. What kind of clothing is very expensive?

   a. T-shirts and sweaters

   b. second-hand clothing

   c. clothes in solid colors

   d. formal clothing

5. Why are a sweater and a skirt better than a dress?

   _____

6. What is a navy-blue jacket called? _____

 ## Let's Read More!

Looking for Quality

How can a shopper be sure to find good-quality clothes? Here is some important information about clothing to remember when you shop:

1. Read labels and tags carefully.

   a. Is the clothing washable? It is easy to take care of washable clothes.

   b. Is the clothing wash and wear? That means it needs little ironing.

    c. Is the clothing permanent press? That means it needs no ironing.

    d. Do the clothes need hand washing? Hand washing is extra work!

    e. Does the clothing need dry cleaning? Dry cleaning means extra cost.

2. Check the clothing for quality.

    a. Check the brand. Each item has a label. The label tells the "brand" of clothes; the brand tells you who made the clothing. Some brands are very good quality. Other brands are not such good quality. Read the label. Does the brand mean good quality? Is it the store's own brand?

    b. Is the material cut straight? If it isn't cut straight, it won't look good for a long time.

    c. Is the sewing even? Is the sewing strong? Can you see the sewing from the outside?

    d. Is the cloth good quality? Is it strong? Does it look clean? Is the material colorfast? Colorfast material will keep its color. It will not fade easily.

    e. Will the clothing shrink? Look at the label carefully. Does the label say anything about shrinking? Shrinking makes clothes too small.

    f. Children's clothes must be strong. Check the buttons and buttonholes. Is the sewing good? Will the clothes last for a season?

    g. Look at the inside of clothing. The quality is easy to see from the inside.

Let's Practice!

Reading Labels

According to the law, all new clothes must have labels with washing instructions. Here are some examples. What do they mean? Complete the sentences by writing the words in the blanks.

1.

> MACHINE WASH COLD
> NORMAL CYCLE
> BLEACH NEEDED
> LINE OR TUMBLE DRY ON COOL SETTING
> USE COOL IRON

    a. You want this item to be clean. So, you must _____

       it in a washing _____ .

    b. Use _____ water, not hot.

    c. This item does not need gentle cycle. Use the _____
       cycle.

    d. This item is white, and the cloth is strong. So, you must use

       _____ .

    e. Dry it on a _____ or in a dryer.

    f. If you use a dryer, the temperature must be _____ ,
       not hot.

    g. The iron must be _____ too.

2.

> HAND WASH
> WARM WATER
> MILD SOAP
> DRIP DRY
> MED IRON

    a. Do not wash this item in a _____ .

    b. The water must be _____ , not cold.

c. Strong soap will hurt the cloth, so use _____ .

d. Do not dry this item in a _____ .

e. The iron's temperature must be medium, not _____

and not _____ .

3.

WASH BY HAND OR MACHINE,
WASH TEMP 50 DEGREES CELSIUS

TUMBLE DRY, COOL TEMP
REMOVE AT ONCE

DO NOT WRING OR TWIST

LITTLE OR NO IRONING

DO NOT USE BLEACH

a. Wash this item of clothing in _____ water, not cold.

b. The water temperature for warm water is _____ .

c. You can use a washing _____ , or you can wash it

by _____ .

d. In a dryer, the air must be _____ , not hot.

e. Do not _____ the clothing in the dryer.

f. Do not twist or _____ the clothing.

g. You do not need to _____ this item of clothing.

h. Bleach is _____ necessary. Bleach can ruin cloth
and change the color.

4.

> MACHINE WASH WARM, GENTLE CYCLE
>
> WASH DARK COLORS AND PRINTS SEPARATELY
>
> WASH WHITES AND LIGHT COLORS WITH LIKE COLORS
>
> TUMBLE DRY LOW COOL SETTING
>
> REMOVE PROMPTLY FROM WATER
>
> DO NOT USE BLEACH ON COLORS OR PRINTS
>
> DO NOT USE HOT IRON

a. Wash this item in warm _____ .

b. Do not mix _____ clothes and colored clothes.
   Wash them separately.

c. In a dryer, the air must not be _____ .

d. Bleach will hurt _____ and _____ .

e. A _____ iron will also ruin this item of clothing.

Let's Think!

Some Problems in Buying Clothing

A. **Irene Williams is a teacher. Mrs. Williams has been thinking about her wardrobe. She needs the following pieces of clothing for winter:**

- a coat
- a wool cape
- three sweaters
- three skirts (to match the sweaters)
- three pairs of pants (also to match the sweaters)
- three blouses (to match the skirts and pants)
- two formal dresses
- some underwear

Mrs. Williams cannot buy all these clothes. Please help her.

1. To buy everything on her list, how much money would

   Mrs. Williams need? _____

How much does a coat cost? _____

How much does a wool cape cost? _____

How much does a sweater cost? _____

How much does a skirt cost? _____

How much does a pair of pants cost? _____

How much does a blouse cost? _____

How much does a formal dress cost? _____

How much does underwear cost? _____

2. Do you think that she understands about mixing and matching? Why? _____

3. What clothing doesn't she need? _____

4. How much money can you help her to save? _____

B. Matthew Sawyer is a young businessman. He plans to spend his money carefully. For each work day of the year, he can spend $5 (five dollars) for clothing.

1. There are about 250 work days a year. How much can Mr. Sawyer spend on clothing? He can spend…

   a. $50.   c. $1,250.

   b. $500.   d. $2,000.

2. A good suit costs $250. If Matt wears it 100 times a year, how much does it cost each time?

   a. $2.50   c. $40.

   b. $4.   d. $10.

3. How many suits can Matt afford? (He must buy other clothes, too!)

   a. one   c. three

   b. two   d. four

4. Matt wants to buy another suit. What will you tell him? (Circle all the right answers.)

   a. You can buy another suit.

   b. You can't afford to buy a suit.

   c. You can buy a solid color jacket and two pairs of pants.

   d. Don't buy lots of suits.

   e. Mix and match!

   f. Get a navy blue blazer.

   g. You already have a nice suit.

5. Matt bought a new suit, but he also needs two new pairs of shoes for work. Shoes cost $70 a pair. How much can he still spend on clothes?

   a. $1,420   c. $580

   b. $860   d. $670

6. What other clothes does Matt need? _____

   _____

7. How much money can he spend on other clothes? _____

Let's Practice!

Comparing Two Things

Circle the right answer.

1. Which price is lower?

   a. $11.98   b. twelve dollars

2. Which color is lighter?

   a. white   b. brown

3. Which color is darker?

   a. red   b. black

4. Which is cheaper?

   a. a jacket ($145) and a pair of pants ($48)

   b. a suit ($220)

5. Which is cooler?
   a. forty degrees Celsius   b. 50° C

6. Which is bigger?
   a. size 8H   b. size 10

7. Why does some clothing shrink?
   a. Someone washed it in hot water.
   b. It dripped dry on a line.

 ## Let's Talk!

Bring clothing catalogs to class. Look at the cost of clothing with a group of friends. Talk about the items in the catalog. Check the cost of different items of clothing. Then look at the questions and write answers with your classmates.

1. How much does each person in your group spend on clothing a year?
2. How much of your money (%, or percentage) do you spend for clothes?
3. Choose clothes of all necessary kinds for a whole year. How much would this wardrobe cost you?

 ## Let's Practice!

A. Find the Different Word

Which word is not a part of the category? All the words except one in each list belong to one category. Find the word. Draw a circle around it. Then ask the question: What is the category?

1.	small	large	size	big
2.	feet	foot	inch	
3.	blouse	pants	dress	skirt
4.	sweater	blouse	shirt	skirt
5.	sweater	blazer	jacket	coat
6.	cotton	wool	linen	flax

7.	animal	leather	cloth	fur
8.	weave	wear	spin	sew
9.	measurement	style	size	
10.	summer	winter	season	fall
11.	color	style	size	spin
12.	dresses	pants	suits	
13.	warm	cool	dry	hot
14.	variety	brand	label	
15.	fashion	quality	style	
16.	spinner	weaver	tailor	dryer
17.	permanent press	wash-and-wear	tumble-dry	
18.	good quality	ready-made	well-made	

B. Practice with New Words

Find a word to fit in each blank.

1. once = at _____ time and only then

2. The weather isn't warm, and it isn't cold. It's _____ .

3. That boy is 15 years old. So, he is a _____ . That girl is twelve years old. She is not a _____ yet, but she will be a _____ (same word) soon.

4. Bryan is not short. He is a very _____ man.

5. We don't need it. It is _____ .

6. He is 53" tall. Fifty-three inches is his _____ .

7. dark blue = _____ blue

8. big = _____

9. The four seasons are spring, summer, _____ , and _____ .

10. Styles are different from year to year. Last year's clothes can be

    _____ .

11. _____ clothes are for special times. Men wear black
    suits, and women wear long dresses.

12. very often = _____

13. The dress is one color only. The dress is a _____
    color.

14. You can wash these clothes. They are _____ .

15. These clothes are very good _____ . They are a
    very good brand. The cloth is good. The sewing is good. The style
    looks good too.

16. _____ clothes keep their color.

17. You work on Mondays, don't you? Monday is a _____ .
    day for you, isn't it?

18. You want white clothes to stay white. You use _____ .

19. Take it out of the water. _____ it from the water.

20. There are many different kinds and sizes! There is a

    _____ .

21. Read the label on these clothes. Can I _____ them?
    (use an iron on them).

22. Little silkworms make _____ fibers.

23. Soft white fibers come from the _____ plant.

24. Sheep give us _____ for warm winter clothes.

25. To get the water from clothes when you wash them, you put them

    in a _____ or _____ them on a line.

26. Fur comes from animal _____ , and

    _____ does too.

Step 11

Before You Read

1. Where do you buy your food?
2. How often do you go food shopping?
3. Why is it important to compare prices of food in different stores?

Spending Money on Food

1   Food is a large part of every person's budget. After all, we have to eat. Is it possible to eat good food on a low budget? Is it possible to eat well and not spend much money? Can a person buy good food cheaply? How does a
5   person buy food wisely? What makes a person a good shopper?

      There are some ways to eat well on little money. First, be wise and make a budget on how to spend all your money. Also make a food budget. How much can you
10   afford to spend each week? Can you make menus, or food plans, for a week at a time? Such careful planning is a good idea, and it will save you money on your food budget.

      To begin with, careful food shoppers make shopping lists. At the store, they use these lists. Sometimes there are
15   good prices for some products, but some other products are often very expensive. So, a wise shopper makes changes in the list at the store. Perhaps the shopper planned to buy one vegetable, but the price for that vegetable is high. Then he or she buys a less expensive vegetable. An intelligent
20   shopper checks prices and thinks before buying.

      Wise shoppers check the newspaper advertisements for "food specials." Food specials are products on sale. Before going to the store, these people check their cupboards. They check their refrigerators, too. What food is already
25   there? Some foods do not spoil; they keep for a long time. Other foods get old and do not taste good. They lose some of their food quality too. An intelligent shopper thinks before buying. What sale products are necessary? Will they spoil?

30   Another question is how much the family will eat. Wise shoppers are careful to buy the right amount of food. It is not good to buy too much food. Too much food can become expensive. Why? Because the family seldom eats it all, and it is thrown away. Food in the garbage is a waste

35 of money.

    Wise shoppers check the dates on food labels too. They buy fresh new food. Old food is not good in quality. A good example is bread. It gets old quickly. Another example is fish. This food spoils fast. Who wants to eat

40 bad food? Who will eat spoiled food? Of course, some other foods do not spoil. Rice is a good example of this kind of food. You can buy large amounts of rice without a problem. Wait until a sale to buy a large bag of rice. Rice keeps for a long time in a cool dry place.

45   There is another way to save money on your food budget. Wise shoppers check prices. They check the amount and the cost. How much does each ounce or each pound of a food cost? A good shopper is careful. He or she gets the most for the money. A wise shopper can cut food

50 costs by careful shopping!

    [A good shopper knows the following information: An ounce is twenty-eight (28) grams. A pound is about half a kilogram. There are sixteen (16) ounces in a pound.]

Let's Learn from the Reading!

Read these questions and try to answer them. You can look in the reading for the answers if you need to.

1. What is a menu? _____

2. Why is a week of menus a good idea? (Circle all the right answers.)

    a. The shopper can buy all the necessary food at one time.

    b. The meals can include the foods on sale.

    c. There are no new foods on the menu.

    d. The shopper does not need to think about food and menus more than one time.

    e. The shopper knows how much to buy.

3. Why do good shoppers check newspapers? (Circle all the right answers.)

    a. for special sales at supermarkets

    b. to save money on special prices

    c. for news

    d. to find out about the variety of foods at the stores

    e. for the address of a store

4. What is a budget?

    a. a kind of food

    b. a menu for a week

    c. a plan for spending money

    d. other products at the supermarket

5. Why do intelligent shoppers check prices and amounts carefully? (Circle all the right answers.)

    a. Smaller amounts of food usually cost more.

    b. Some stores are much more expensive than other stores.

    c. They want to understand labels.

    d. They want to save money on food.

    e. They buy only what they need and will use.

6. On some foods, like milk, there is a month and day. Why are these dates on some packages of food and not on others?

    a. Some foods get old and spoil. Then they are not good to eat.

    b. You can buy some foods only on those days.

    c. Stores throw away old foods.

    d. Stores make food on that date.

7. Which foods can spoil in one week? (Circle all the right answers.)

   a. meat

   b. fish

   c. rice

   d. sugar

   e. bread

   f. ice cream

   g. fruit

   h. oil

   i. canned foods

   j. frozen foods

8. "Wise shoppers can cut food costs." This sentence means that…

   a. they spend more money.

   b. they spend less money.

9. Which of these foods will keep? (Circle all the right answers.)

   a. canned fish

   b. frozen vegetables

   c. a bag of sugar

   d. fresh vegetables

   e. ice cream

   f. canned milk

   g. a loaf of bread

   h. a bag of rice

   i. chicken

   j. fruit

   k. a carton of milk

   l. fresh meat

10. Why do good shoppers check their cupboards and refrigerators before going shopping? _____

11. Which word means "become bad so someone cannot eat it"?

    a. spend

    b. check

    c. save

    d. spoil

12. What does "to get the most for your money" mean?

    a. to buy too much

    b. to spend money wisely

    c. to throw away

    d. to keep

 **Let's Read More!**

Best Buys

1   There are always sales in supermarkets. Items on sale are cheaper than usual. These items are good buys for a week. Sometimes sale items are canned foods. Sometimes they are frozen foods or meats. Canned food does not

5   spoil, and frozen foods keep a long time. So, buy lots of these items if you have a place to keep them. It is a good idea to buy these sale items. Buy as much as your family will want to eat in a few months.

There are often different package sizes. Read the labels

10   on the packages carefully. Check the price of one pound. Usually the price for each pound is the lowest in the biggest package. So, usually the biggest package is the best buy.

Some supermarkets sell food in bulk. Bulk foods are in

15   big boxes or bins, not in packages. The customer puts the food in a bag. There is very little cost for the bag. There is no cost for advertisement. So, bulk foods are a lot cheaper. Most bulk foods are foods that keep well (like rice and

20   sugar).

What kinds of stores sell food in bulk? Almost all health food stores do. These stores also sell natural foods, so their food is often very good quality. They usually sell vitamins and books about nutrition too. Some of their

25   prices are usually a little higher than the prices at the supermarkets. Some people are happy to pay more for natural foods of high quality.

Many people do not like to shop, and others need to shop fast. Such people go to supermarkets. Supermarkets
30 make everything easy for their customers. So, big super-markets do not sell many bulk foods. Most supermarket food is in packages. Many customers go to supermarkets for that reason, the convenience.

Cooperative stores usually sell bulk foods. The same
35 customers come to a cooperative store every week to shop because the shoppers at a cooperative store own the store. They call their store a "co-op." The food at co-ops is always on sale.

Here is a summary of ways to save money on food:

1. Buy foods on sale.
2. Keep a supply of canned or frozen sale foods.
3. Buy large amounts of foods that you can keep, when the price is low.
4. Buy bulk foods.
5. Become a co-op customer.

Let's Practice!

A. Fact and Reason

In this exercise, there are some facts on the left. On the right, there are reasons. Match the facts and the reasons. Use the correct reason to explain each fact. Then you can make a long sentence. Write the fact and then *because* and then the reason.

FACT + *because* + REASON _____

1. Wise shoppers plan   _____ they own the store.
   menus because…

2. Supermarkets do not sell   __1__ they can save money.
   much bulk food because…

3. It is usually a good idea   _____ they want to make
   to buy the larger sizes   shopping easy for
   because…   their customers.

4. Bulk foods are cheaper   _____ they sell only
   because…   natural foods.

5. Co-op customers always shop _____ they are cheaper.
   at the co-op because…

6. Health food stores have   _____ they do not have
   high prices because…   expensive packages.

Now write the sentences here:

1. _Wise shoppers plan menus because they can save money._

2. _____

3. _____

4. _____

5. _____

6. _____

B. Find the Word

Fill in the blanks.

How do wise shoppers make shopping lists?

They use the advertisements in the _____ .

They write a shopping _____ of necessary things.

They check to see what foods they have. If there is no milk in the

_____ , they write "milk" on their shopping _____ .

C. Good Shopping Rules

Here are four good rules for shoppers. Read the rules and answer the questions. More than one answer is right! (Circle all the right answers.)

Rule 1: DO NOT GO SHOPPING HUNGRY! Why is this rule a good one?

  a. You will not be strong. You will need help to do the shopping.

  b. You will buy unnecessary things.

  c. You will waste money on food to eat NOW.

  d. You will be a slow shopper.

  e. You won't follow your own rules for shopping.

Rule 2: SHOP ONLY ONCE A WEEK! Why is this a good rule?

  a. You will save time.

  b. You will plan your menus.

  c. You will buy foods on sale.

  d. You will have fun at the store.

  e. You will learn to think before you go to the store.

  f. You will check your cupboards and refrigerator.

  g. You won't waste as much food.

Rule 3: PLAN ACCORDING TO A BUDGET! How does shopping only once a week help your budget?

  a. You will spend too much.

  b. You will buy only sale foods.

  c. You will not buy unnecessary foods.

  d. You will plan carefully and cut costs.

  e. You will get old food.

Rule 4: MAKE A SHOPPING LIST AND BUY ONLY THOSE FOODS. A shopping list saves money because…

  a. you don't have money.

  b. you can even save time.

  c. you do not buy unnecessary things.

  d. you waste money on necessary foods.

D. Super Store and Super Prices

Can you find the information to answer these questions on the advertisement? Write your answers in the blanks.

1. The name of the store is _____ .

2. The store hours are _____ .

3. The store address is _____ .

4. The price of a dozen eggs is _____ .

5. The cost of low-fat cheese is _____ .

6. The fruits that are on sale are _____ ,
   _____ , and _____ .

7. The grade of eggs on sale is _____ .

8. The size of canned juice on sale is _____ .

9. How many days is this sale? _____

10. What produce is on sale?

_____

11. Why is Wednesday a good day to shop?

_____

12. Which is more expensive, chicken or ground beef?

_____

13. The store has a special saying: "Super Store — Super Prices."
    What does it mean?
    a. Our prices are very high.
    b. We have a wonderful store.
    c. We sell good food at good prices.
    d. Our store is more than just a supermarket.

E. Category

Which word is not a part of the category? Find the different word and
circle it. What is the category?

1. buy	sell	shop	supermarket
2. cupboard	table	refrigerator	freezer
3. frozen	fresh	canned	
4. menu	store	supermarket	
5. shopping	list	menu	advertisement
6. wise	good	careful	intelligent
7. cheese	pizza	eggs	milk
8. pound	possible	ounce	dozen
9. expensive	price	cost	
10. eggs	juice	milk	

F. Small, Medium, Large

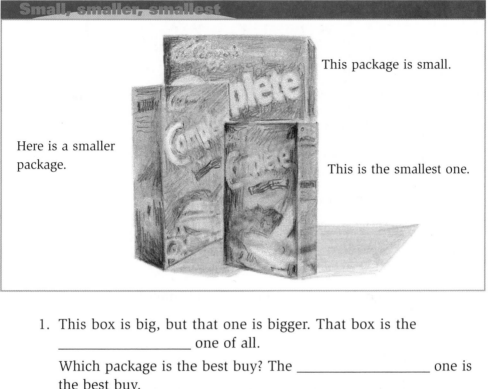

Small, smaller, smallest

This package is small.

Here is a smaller package.

This is the smallest one.

1. This box is big, but that one is bigger. That box is the
   _____ one of all.

   Which package is the best buy? The _____ one is
   the best buy.

2. The small package costs as much as the medium and the large

   packages. The _____ package is not a good buy.

3. These fruits do not look fresh. These fruits look a little bit

   _____ than those. But this fruit here looks like the

   _____ of all.

4. Don't buy milk with an old date. You want a new date. Buy the

   milk with the _____ date.

5. Last week, we spent fifty-five dollars ($55) on food. That cost was

   low. We spent $65 two weeks ago. Today, we spent only $50. This

   week's food cost the _____ all.

G. Use Your New Words

Practice with new words. Use them in the sentences in the exercise.

advertisements	amount	budget	bulk
cheaply	cupboard	customer	date	dozen
freezer	frozen	good	menu	ounces	possible
price	refrigerator	rule	sale	saying
seldom	shopper	slow	spoil	wise

1. Who shops in a store? A _____ does.

2. What is a meal plan? It is a _____ .

3. Where do people keep canned food? In the _____ .

4. Where do people keep fresh food like milk? In the

 _____ .

5. Where do people keep frozen food? In the _____ .

6. "Super Store—Super Prices." This is an example of an

 _____ .

7. If food gets old, it will probably _____ .

8. Sixteen _____ makes one pound.

9. The cost of an item is its _____ .

10. Twelve of an item is one _____ .

11. not very often = _____

12. Food not in packages is in _____ . You put it in a bag at the store.

13. the month, day, and year = the _____

14. Think and plan. Then you can be a _____ shopper.

15. not expensively = _____

16. You can find _____ in newspapers for special sales.

17. A pound is an _____ of food.

18. Eggs are cheap this week. They are on _____ .

19. You can do it. = It's _____ for you to do it.

20. He always shops there. He's a _____ .

21. She isn't a fast shopper. She's a _____ shopper. (She shops slowly.)

22. This meat is hard and cold, like ice. This meat is

_____ .

23. She thinks and shops at the same time. So, she is a

_____ shopper. (She spends her money wisely.)

24. "Don't shop hungry." = an example of a shopping

_____

25. He can spend $8 a day for food. It's the amount on his

_____ .

◇| Let's Talk!

Let's talk about food. With your class or with a classmate, think about the names for foods. You will make a list of different kinds of foods. Write your list here.

_____   _____

_____   _____

_____   _____

_____   _____

Now let's put the foods into categories.

Our first group is grains. This category includes rice and bread. What other foods are probably in this group?

_____	_____
_____	_____
_____	_____
_____	_____
_____	_____

The second group is fruits and vegetables. These are fresh foods. Many people grow vegetables in their gardens. Some people have fruit trees, too. Do you know the names of any fruits and vegetables? Are there some in your list? Write the names here.

_____	_____
_____	_____
_____	_____
_____	_____
_____	_____

The third group includes milk, eggs, meat, and fish. What other foods on your list could be in this group?

_____	_____
_____	_____
_____	_____
_____	_____
_____	_____

The last group includes sweet foods and oils. Name some foods in this group. Do you have some of these foods on your list?

_____ _____

_____ _____

_____ _____

_____ _____

_____ _____

Let's Write!

Make a menu for a lunch for yourself and a friend. Plan the shopping list. There will not be much time to make the lunch, so plan carefully!

Menu
Grain:_____
_____
Vegetables:_____
_____
Meat group: _____
_____
Something to drink: _____
_____
Fruit: _____
_____

Let's Find Out About You!

Complete the paragraph.

My friend _____ and I are planning

a lunch for ourselves. We plan to have _____

_____ .

We will buy _____

_____ at the store.

We have one hour to make our lunch.

Special Project

Go to a food store. Check the prices of some foods.

1. How much is bread? _____

   Is all bread the same price? _____

   Why or why not? _____

   _____

2. Check out the fresh foods. Write the names of five vegetables and five fruits.

   _____   _____

   _____   _____

   _____   _____

   _____   _____

   _____   _____

3. Can you find any bulk foods in the store? If so, what kinds of foods can you buy in bulk?

_____   _____

_____   _____

_____   _____

_____   _____

_____   _____

4. Can you buy frozen vegetables there? _____

   Does the store have frozen fruits? _____

   Does the store sell frozen meats? _____

Step 12

Before You Read

1. What causes most fires?
2. Where do fires start?
3. How can you keep yourself safe from fires?

The Danger of Fires

1   Fires are a great danger to people, animals, and buildings. A fire can happen anywhere, at any time. There are many fires every year. These fires burn forests, destroy homes, kill animals, and hurt people. Most of the time, something
5   can be done to prevent these terrible disasters and the great damage. Of course, we need fire for heat, for cooking, and for many other reasons. However, fire must be kept under control. It is important to know how to control fire. Then fire works for us and not against us.

10   The first important fact is to understand fires. Three things are necessary for a fire. First, a fire needs fuel. Fuel is something like wood, oil, and gas—things that burn easily. We put these fuels in our furnaces and burn them for heat. Furnaces make our homes warm. There are other fuels, too.
15   Sometimes we do not understand that they are truly fuels. For example, old newspapers are a kind of fuel. Oily cloths (that people use for cleaning) burn easily too. Some chemicals can also burn and even start fires. Matches have chemicals on the tips of the sticks. All these fuels can
20   cause fires.

The second important fact about fire is the need for heat. Without heat, there is no fire. The heat of a match starts a fire, but heat collects in some places in a house. For example, electricity is heat. Old electrical equipment
25   (especially old wires) can start fires. Oily cloths (rags) hold heat. The heat collects in a pile of oily rags. These rags can start to burn—if they get hot enough. So oily rags near a furnace or other kind of heater can easily start a fire. It is important to remember that the sun is also a source of heat.

30   A person should not leave oily rags in a pile in the sun either. They can start to burn.

Air is also necessary for a fire because air contains oxygen. Oxygen makes things burn. It is also necessary for a fire. Air is the third thing necessary for a fire to burn.

35   What causes a fire? A match is not necessary. If there is fuel and if there is heat and if there is air with oxygen, there can be a fire. The right amounts of these things make a fire.

How can people prevent fires? They can be careful with heat. They can put fuel in a safe place. They can keep fuels

40   from air. For example, a person should not put newspapers near a furnace. They could start to burn. A person should put oily cloths inside a can with a cover. Then there will not be much air near the oily cloths. That can should be far from heat. Then a fire cannot start.

45   There are no fires without fuel, heat, and oxygen. If you keep these three things separate, you can avoid the danger of fires.

Let's Learn from the Reading!

1. What can fire destroy?

   _____

   _____

2. How can fire hurt people? (Circle all the right answers.)
   a. It can burn people's houses.
   b. It can burn in the furnace.
   c. It can cause electricity.
   d. It can kill people.
   e. It can burn trees and crops in their fields.
   f. It can cost people a lot of money.

3. What are some fuels that people burn in furnaces?

_____

_____

4. What three things are necessary for a fire?

_____   _____   _____

5. Why is air necessary for a fire?
   a. Air is a kind of fuel. It burns very well.
   b. Air is heat. We need to have heat for a fire.
   c. Air has oxygen in it. Oxygen is necessary for a fire.
   d. Air is a kind of fuel.

6. How can a person prevent fires? (Circle all the right answers.)
   a. Keep old newspapers.
   b. Think about safety.
   c. Do not use your furnace.
   d. Don't leave a pile of oily rags in the sun.
   e. Keep air, fuel, and heat separate.
   f. Put oily rags in a can with a cover.
   g. Store fuels far from sources of heat like a furnace or stove.

 Let's Read More!

Be Ready for a Fire

1   People hear a lot of information about fires. They read
in newspapers about fires, and they see reports about fires
on television. People know about the dangers of fire.
However, not many people prepare for a fire. Not many
5 people are ready for one, because fires happen to other
people.

However, some people work hard to prevent fires. They make their homes safe. They are ready to fight against fire. For example, they know how to use a fire
10   extinguisher. They can put out a little fire fast. They are even ready for a big fire.

How can a family prepare for a fire? Here are some ways:

They must put smoke detectors in their house. A smoke detector is an alarm. Smoke from a fire causes the alarm
15   to go off. The alarm makes a  loud sound. The sound tells everyone to leave the house. It is a warning about a possible fire in the house.

They make escape plans. They know all the ways out of
20   the house. If there is a fire, everyone follows the escape plan and goes out of the house. They all know to meet in one place outside of the house. If someone is not there, they will know if someone is still in the house. Then no one will go back into the house to look for someone. Part of an escape
25   plan is to check all the windows. Do the windows all open easily? Can the children open the windows to get out? Do they need ladders to get out of high windows?

They buy fire extinguishers and learn to use them. They teach the young people in the family to use them too.
30   They practice for a fire. They have fire drills because fire drills teach children about fire safety. Everyone in the family should know these fire rules:

- DO NOT OPEN A HOT DOOR! There could be a fire behind a hot door. Do not open it. The fire
35   can grow quickly if you open the door. Opening the door adds more oxygen to the fire!
- STAY CLOSE TO THE FLOOR! Smoke can be more dangerous than fire. Fire uses up the oxygen in the

air. People die without air. The best air is near the
40 floor because smoke rises.

- STOP! DROP! AND ROLL! Fire cannot burn without
air. What if a person's hair or clothes start to burn?
What should that person do?
First, STOP! Do not run! The fire will burn faster
45 because of more air, so stop!
DROP! Fall to the floor.
Then ROLL! Turning over and over will make the
fire go out. Put a blanket or a rug around you to
keep air away from the fire that may still be on you.

50 A fire can happen anywhere. It is wise to expect a fire.
A wise family is ready at all times.

Remember: There are many possible causes for fires in
every home. Every home has a stove. Every home has
matches. Every home has possible electrical problems.
55 Every year someone should check the furnace and the
stove. This equipment should be clean. It should work
well and safely. Many things in a home can burn. Keep
flammable things away from heat. Teach children to be
careful too. Teach them the danger of matches.

Let's Learn from the Reading!

1. Why is an escape plan a good idea? An escape plan is a good
   idea because...
   a. the people are ready to get out of the house fast.
   b. it gets hot during a fire.
   c. they need to have fire drills.
   d. then the children can open the windows.

2. How can fire drills help children prepare for a fire?

   a. Children like to open windows.

   b. Children need smoke detectors.

   c. Children need practice with escape plans.

   d. Children must not know about the dangers of fires.

3. It is important to buy a fire extinguisher. It is more important to learn how to use it right away. Why? You need to learn how to use a fire extinguisher. Then...

   a. you can put out a fire.

   b. you can't put out any fires.

   c. you can get hurt.

   d. you can put a smoke detector in your house.

4. What is another name for a home fire alarm?

   a. fire extinguisher

   b. smoke detector

   c. escape plan

   d. electrical problems

5. What are some other fire dangers in a house? (Circle all the right answers.)

   a. oily rags

   b. fireplaces

   c. windows

   d. kitchen stoves

   e. smoke detectors

   f. electrical equipment

   g. furnaces

   h. stores

   i. matches

   j. books

   k. fire extinguishers

   l. curtains near a source of heat

6. "They checked the house, but there was no problem." This sentence means the same as...

   a. They checked the house, so there was no problem.

   b. They checked the house, and there was no problem.

   c. They checked the house. Then there was no problem.

   d. They checked the house. However, there was no problem.

7. Which of these things is a source of heat? (Circle all the right answers.)

   a. the sun

   b. a kitchen stove

   c. a ladder

   d. a furnace

   e. a window

   f. a fire extinguisher

   g. electrical equipment

 Let's Think About It!

The *Stop, Drop, and Roll* rule to stop yourself from burning saves many people's lives. Which of the three things necessary for a fire (fuel, heat, air) is the reason the rule works? Explain your answer.

What makes a fire extinguisher work to stop a fire?

Which of the three things necessary for a fire (fuel, heat, air) is the easiest to stop if a fire is burning?

Let's Read More!

Escaping from a Fire

1   Pat wakes up in the night and hears a funny sound. She also smells smoke. She goes to her bedroom door and puts her hand on it. It feels hot. There might be a fire on the other side of the door. She does not open the door.

5   Why not? The fire is very near it. She goes out the window and shouts in a loud voice. She calls for help and warns the other members of the family. She climbs out of her window and helps them to get out of other windows. She follows the rules for escaping from a fire.

10   What are the rules for a fire in a home? What should you do in case of fire? First, quickly wake the rest of the family.

Then tell everyone to get out of the house fast. Warn them about keeping doors closed. Next, call the emergency number; in North America, it is 911. The fire department
15   will come to help right away. If possible, find the fire and put it out with a fire extinguisher.

    It is a good idea to have plans for escape from a fire. It is also a good idea to practice with the family. Fire drills are especially important for small children because they
20   forget easily. Another danger is that they are naturally afraid of fires. Young children will want to hide from a fire. That's why they often go under a bed. The air stays clear for the longest time near the floor. However, it is better for children to know how to get out of the house fast.
25   Someone might not find them under a bed. Frequent fire drills make emergency action easy to remember. Also, remember: Beds are flammable, and they burn fast. Fire can burn children under a bed.

Let's Learn from the Reading!

1. Why is a hot door a danger sign?
   a. The fire is very near.
   b. There is a lot of smoke.
   c. Doors burn first.
   d. Fire extinguishers cannot help doors.

2. Why is under a bed a good place for children in a fire?
   a. It is cool there.
   b. There is air near the floor.
   c. Mattresses do not burn.
   d. Fire cannot find children there.

3. Why is under the bed a dangerous place for children in a fire?

   a. It is hot there.

   b. There is no air there.

   c. Mattresses burn.

   d. Fire cannot find children there.

4. Why is an escape plan a good idea?

   a. You want to get everyone out of the house safely.

   b. You don't need a fire extinguisher.

   c. You don't have smoke detectors.

   d. You don't have to ask someone for help.

5. What is a fire drill?

   a. a kind of smoke detector

   b. practice for a fire

   c. some electrical equipment

   d. a kind of fire extinguisher

Let's Practice!

A. More About Fires

Picture One shows an important tool. It is a fire extinguisher.

1. How many fire extinguishers does a family need? _____

2. Where should there be a fire extinguisher?

   _____ _____

   _____

Picture Two shows the necessary conditions for a fire. There must be three things.

They are _____ ,

_____ , and _____ .

B. Category

Which word is not a part of the category? Find the different word and circle it. What is the category?

1.	gasoline	water	gas	
2.	prevent	avoid	stop	air
3.	home	apartment	house	building
4.	stove	garbage	heater	furnace
5.	heater	furnace	stove	table
6.	cloth	can	rag	
7.	oil	emergency	alarm	
8.	fire alarm	fire extinguisher	smoke detector	
9.	oil	room	wood	gas
10.	air	water	fuel	heat
11.	table	washing machine	refrigerator	freezer
12.	fire	fire drill	practice	
13.	but	however	so	
14.	prevent	problem	protect	
15.	oily cloth	old newspapers	hot door	
16.	heat	oxygen	fire	
17.	fast	quickly	hot	slowly
18.	save	stop	roll	drop

Let's Talk!

Think about these examples. Are there any safety problems? What can you do to make them safer? Talk your answers over with a classmate. Do you have the same ideas?

1. The Allens' house is warm because of a big furnace. The furnace is in a small room on the first floor. There is room in that small room, so the Allens keep old newspapers there. They store things for cleaning there too.

2. The Smiths' house has three floors. The kitchen and living room are on the first floor. There is a fireplace in the living room. On the second floor (the second story), there is one bedroom and a television room. The children's bedrooms are on the top floor. The Smiths have a smoke detector in the kitchen.

3. There are three young children in the Johnson family. They like to play with interesting things. They like to play near the fireplace in the living room. There are matches, wood, and paper near the fireplace.

 Let's Practice with Pronouns!

Look at these sentences. The underlined words in each line mean the same thing. But they have different uses.

Sam and Ellen are cleaning their home library. They are putting Sam's books in one place and Ellen's book in another place. Their children, Mark and Anna, have books too. Their books go in separate places too.

Ellen: Whose book is this one?
Sam: It's my book. This one is mine too.
Ellen: Whose book is this one?
Sam: Is it our book? It can't be one of our family's books.
Ellen: Maybe it's Anna's book.
Sam: It could be hers. Her books are here.
Ellen: And this one is Mark's.
Sam: No, that's not his. His book about sports is blue.

Rules:
Use *my* before a noun. Use *mine* without a noun.
Use *her* before a noun. Use *hers* without a noun.
Use *our* before a noun and *ours* without a noun.
Use *his* with or without a noun.

First read this paragraph about Ellen.

Ellen is showing her new house to her friend, Kathy Smith. Ellen says, "This is our living room. And here is my kitchen. It's my favorite room in the house. Many of my things are here. Let's go up to the bedrooms. This is Anna's room. Her things are in this room. Here are some of her old toys. And this room is Mark's. He keeps his things in his room. Here is Mark's tennis racket. Sam and I have a large room, but it has all our books in it. It is too small for all our things.

Now write the paragraph over again. Fill in the blanks with *my, mine, our, ours, her, hers,* or *his.* There are some important changes.

Ellen is showing _____ new house to a friend of

_____ , Kathy Smith. Ellen says, "This is the living

room. And here is _____ kitchen. It's _____

favorite room in the house. Many things of _____ are

here. Let's go up to the bedrooms. This is Anna's room.

Important things of _____ are in this room, like

_____ old toys. And this room is Mark's. He keeps

_____ things in this room of _____ . Here is

Mark's tennis racket. Sam and I have a large room, but it

has all _____ books in it. It is too small for all these

things of _____ .

Let's Find Out About You!

What information do you know about fire safety?

What do you know about the danger of fires out of control?

Step 13

Before You Read

1. "You are what you eat." Explain what this saying means.

2. What help is there for a person who wants to plan a good diet?

3. What foods are best for a person? Which are the most harmful?

The Importance of Good Health

1　　There is an old saying. "Money can't buy everything." The richest person in the world cannot buy health.

How can a person find good health? Good health comes from good habits. A healthy person eats good food
5　and has good eating habits. A healthy person gets sleep and exercise, too. So if you want to be healthy, always eat good food, drink lots of water, and get exercise every day. Good habits help a person stay healthy.

What is a good diet? The best advice for any good diet
10　is variety. A nutritious diet includes many kinds of foods. Different foods have different food value. For example, every day most people need food from the bread and rice group. The name for these foods is carbohydrates. Carbohydrates give people energy to work.

15　　There are two classes of carbohydrates. One class includes starchy foods like bread, rice, and potatoes. The second class of carbohydrates is the sugar group, a group of foods that contain honey or sugar in them. Cake, ice cream, cookies, and other desserts are in this group. The
20　best kind of carbohydrates are simple ones, like rice and potatoes. Manufactured foods (like cake, white flour, and most chips) can be harmful. Most junk food and almost all sweet foods are "refined carbohydrates." These foods no longer look like the natural foods that they were made from.
25　Food-makers have changed the ingredients in factories, so they are now "manufactured" foods.

A person also needs protein every day. Protein comes from fish, meat, and eggs. There is protein in milk and cheese and some vegetables, too. For example, beans are

30 an important source of vegetable protein. One cup of beans
is enough protein for one person for a day.

A good diet also includes fresh foods. Vegetables and
fruits contain important vitamins and minerals. These
natural chemicals are necessary for good health. We need
35 to get vitamins and minerals from our foods, or else we
must take vitamin pills.

How can you be sure of a good diet? One way is to learn
about food. Learn about protein foods and eat some protein
foods every day. Learn about vitamins and minerals. Learn
40 what foods have lots of vitamins and minerals in them. Eat
some fresh foods every day. Eat good carbohydrates like rice
too. A variety usually makes a good diet. Most people need
foods from each group every day.

Look at the picture of the food pyramid on page 201.
45 There are ideas for a good and balanced diet in the pyramid.

Let's Learn from the Reading!

First read the article, and then answer these questions.

1. What can't money buy? _____

   _____

2. Fish, meat, eggs, milk, cheese, and beans all contain _____ .

3. A balanced diet with different foods has a lot of _____ .

4. How can a person learn about a good diet? _____

   _____

5. Why is variety important for a diet? _____

   _____

6. How can a person find health? _____

_____

Let's Talk!

Answer these questions yourself, and then talk them over with a classmate.

1. Can you plan a good diet? What do you need for a good diet?
2. What are the names of some vegetables?
3. Name other fresh foods, like fruits. Apples are one kind of fruit.

Let's Read More!

Junk Food and Good Snack Foods

1   Because people sometimes get hungry between meals, they like snacks. Sometimes people choose snack foods that don't have much nutrition. This is junk food. *Junk* and *garbage* mean almost the same thing. What is bad

5   about junk food? Is it really *garbage*?

     Junk food usually has a lot of sugar. Usually it also contains too much salt. Most junk food also has a lot of oil in it. It is true that people need to have some salt and some oil in their diets, but most snack foods have too

10   much salt. And the oil is not the best kind of oil, because most manufactured foods are made with the cheapest kind of oil. Furthermore, junk food does not contain many vitamins. It usually does not have much protein, either.

     Children often ask for junk food because they see junk

15   food on TV. They want junk-food snacks between meals. Then they are not hungry at meal time. The junk-food habit is not good for a balanced diet.

There are some natural foods that are good for snacks. For example, fruit, nuts, and vegetables are nutritious
20   snacks. It is true that fruits have sugar in them, and some people should not eat much fruit. However, fruit sugar is a natural sugar. Therefore, fruits are good sources of energy.

Another natural snack, nuts, contain protein, some carbohydrates, and very good natural oil. Raw vegetables
25   are also nutritious. These are not junk food, but they are good snacks.

Let's Learn from the Reading!

1. What do people like to eat between meals? _____

2. What three things does junk food usually contain a lot of?

   _____ _____ _____

3. What does junk food not have much of? _____

4. Why is it important to eat regular meals? _____

   _____

5. Are snacks and junk food always the same? In what ways?

   _____

   _____

6. A balanced diet includes…
   a. lots of junk food.
   b. lots of variety.
   c. no sugar, salt, or oil.
   d. snacks of all kinds.

⊚ Let's Practice!

Let's practice with the names of foods.

1. It is time to learn the names of more foods. First make a list of
   foods. Your teacher could write food names on the board.

   _____   _____

   _____   _____

   _____   _____

   _____   _____

   _____   _____

2. When is an apple a snack?

   _____

   _____

3. When is a cookie dessert?

   _____

   _____

4. Here are some snack foods. Do you know these words? Are some
   of them on your list for number 1? You can ask your teacher or
   a classmate for the meaning. You can also look them up in a
   dictionary. Which of these foods have good food value? Which
   ones are the best snack foods? Write a check next to your answers.

   popcorn _____   peanuts _____

   carrots _____   cookies _____

   oranges _____   fruit _____

   tomatoes _____   celery _____

   raw vegetables _____   pie _____

   potatoes _____   cake _____

   potato chips _____   corn chips _____

   bananas _____   apples _____

   nuts _____   candy _____

Let's Talk!

First answer these questions for yourself. Then work with a classmate.

1. What are some of your favorite snacks?
2. Are your favorite snack foods nutritious? Which ones?
3. Do you eat junk food often?
4. What other kind of food can you eat in place of junk foods?

 Let's Read More!

A Recipe for You

1
SUPER COOKIES

Here is a recipe for cookies. They are called Super Cookies. The recipe tells how to make them. It also tells the ingredients. Ingredients for cookies are foods like sugar, flour, and eggs.
5 These cookies contain protein and a lot of vitamins. That is the reason for their name.

Ingredients:

$\frac{1}{4}$ cup of oil (75 grams)

$\frac{1}{2}$ cup of yogurt (125 grams)

10 1 cup of brown sugar (250 grams)

$\frac{3}{4}$ cup of molasses (180 grams)

2 eggs

1 tablespoon of vanilla [1 T.] (a soup spoon)

First put the oil and yogurt in a bowl. Mix them together
15 with a spoon. Add the brown sugar and molasses. Mix these ingredients well. Add the 2 eggs and mix again. In another bowl, mix these dry ingredients:

1 teaspoon of baking powder [1 t. or 1 tsp.]

1 teaspoon of baking soda [1 t.]

20 $\frac{1}{2}$ teaspoon of salt [$\frac{1}{2}$ t.]

$1^1/_2$ cups of dried powdered milk (with no water)

[$1^1/_2$ c.] (375 grams]

2 cups of flour (sift the flour) (500 grams)

$^3/_4$ cup of wheat germ (180 grams)

25      $^1/_2$ cup of oatmeal (125 grams)

Add the dry ingredients to the first bowl. Mix all the ingredients well. You can also add raisins and nuts. Use a small spoon to make each cookie. Put the dough on a greased pan.

Super Cookies need to bake for about 15 minutes. Bake

30   them in the oven at 325–350 degrees Fahrenheit or 160–175 degrees Celsius. Celsius is the same as Centigrade.

Take them from the oven and let them cool. Then you can enjoy them! They are great!

Let's Learn from the Reading!

Try to answer these questions after you read the article.

1. What does *ingredient* mean? An ingredient is...

    a. something like cookies.

    b. some kind of food in a recipe.

    c. protein and vitamins.

    d. a bowl and a spoon.

2. What is the first dry ingredient on the list? _____

3. How long do the cookies need to bake? _____

    What will happen if they bake longer? _____

4. What other ingredients can you add? _____

    _____

5. Why are these cookies called Super Cookies? _____

    _____

Let's Practice!

Here are some exercises for you to do. You can practice the new words with these exercises.

A. Abbreviations

1. There are some special words and abbreviations in cookbooks. Recipes also leave a lot of words out. Can you guess why? (Circle all the right answers.)

    a. Recipes are old, so they use old English.

    b. Recipes are directions for making food. They must be easy to follow and easy to understand.

    c. Recipes are hard to write.

    d. A person can "read" an abbreviation faster than a word.

2. What are some abbreviations in recipes?

    _____   _____   _____

3. Check the recipe. What do these abbreviations mean?

    1 t. = _____

    1 T. = _____

    $2\frac{1}{2}$ c. = _____

    Here are some more abbreviations. What could they mean?

    50 g = _____

    1 l. = _____

    $\frac{1}{2}$ lb. = _____

    $\frac{1}{2}$ oz. = _____

4. Find some more abbreviations.

    _____

    _____

B. The Food Pyramid

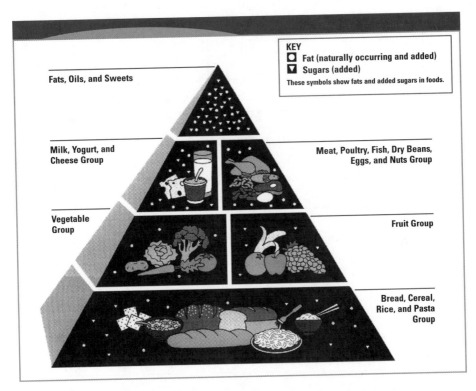

KEY
- ☐ Fat (naturally occurring and added)
- ▼ Sugars (added)

These symbols show fats and added sugars in foods.

Fats, Oils, and Sweets

Milk, Yogurt, and Cheese Group

Meat, Poultry, Fish, Dry Beans, Eggs, and Nuts Group

Vegetable Group

Fruit Group

Bread, Cereal, Rice, and Pasta Group

The picture shows the food pyramid. There are four floors, or levels, to this pyramid. The first floor is carbohydrates. Most people need to eat a lot of carbohydrates (3–5 cups a day, or 500–750 grams of food weight). The next story is fresh foods. A good diet includes $1^1/_2$–$2^1/_2$ cups or 375–625 grams of vegetables and 2 or 3 pieces of fruit. The third level of the pyramid is for the most important food group, proteins. A normal person needs only 3–5 ounces of protein a day. He or she can get the protein from milk, cheese, yogurt, beans, meat, fish, nuts, or eggs. About five ounces of protein (150–200 grams) is enough for most people. Protein is probably the most important food group because it builds muscle. Mothers of new babies and sports players, for example, need more protein, but everyone needs protein because much of the body is muscle! Fats, oils, and sweets are also part of the pyramid. They are at the top. There is natural oil, fat, and sweets in foods, so people don't need more. People should avoid oily, fatty, and sweet manufactured foods.

Write the names of five foods for each category of the pyramid.

Fats, Oils, Sweets

_____   _____

_____   _____

_____

Proteins

_____   _____

_____   _____

_____

Fresh Foods

_____   _____

_____   _____

_____

Carbohydrates

_____   _____

_____   _____

_____

C. Bad Health Habits

The second picture shows a man. He is making many mistakes with his health. He is not exercising. He is _____ television, and he is _____ a cigarette. Cigarettes are dangerous to health. What else is he doing wrong?

_____

_____

D. Good Eating Habits

Today many people want to eat better food and be healthier. They want to eat less fat and less sugar. They want to know how to do it. Here are some ideas.

- Eat fewer manufactured carbohydrates.
- Drink eight glasses of water every day.
- Avoid junk-food snacks.
- Use very little margarine. There is enough natural fat and oil in food.
- Be sure to eat green vegetables and fruits every day. Fresh foods are the most nutritious. They also have a lot of fiber in them. Fiber helps bodies work well.
- Choose more low-fat proteins. Eat beans, fish, or chicken.
- Avoid sugar in desserts. Eat fruit for dessert.

Good food and good diet are not enough. There is another important part of being healthy. A person needs exercise every day. A person also needs to get 7 or 8 hours of sleep every night.

Read these questions and answer them quickly.

1. What is a food pyramid?

    a. a plan for a good diet

    b. a plan for a supermarket

    c. a building in Egypt

    d. a picture of kinds of foods

2. Which category of food is the most important? Why?

    _____

    _____

3. Which protein foods are lowest in fat? _____

    _____

4. How much water should a person drink every day?

    _____

5. What is better to eat than sugar in desserts? _____

    _____

6. Fresh foods include two groups, _____ and

    _____ . These foods are good because of their

    vitamins, their minerals, and their _____ .

Let's Talk!

Read these questions carefully, and then talk with a classmate. Can you answer the questions together?

1. What is good nutrition?

2. Too much weight is a problem. Too little weight is also a problem. Why?

   a. A very thin person is not strong.

   b. A balanced diet is healthful.

   c. Healthy people eat too much food.

   d. Thin people have many problems.

3. What are your favorite recipes?

4. There are many clubs for people on diets. These clubs teach about good nutrition. Are there any clubs in your hometown? What do you know about these clubs?

 Let's Write!

A "serving" of food is about half a cup, or 125 grams. Make a food plan for yourself. Include all the foods in the list.

My Food Plan
BREAKFAST
Carbohydrate: _____
Fresh food: _____
Protein: _____

LUNCH

Carbohydrate: _____

Carbohydrate: _____

Fresh food: _____

Fresh food: _____

Fresh food: _____

Protein: _____

DINNER

Carbohydrate: _____

Carbohydrate: _____

Fresh food: _____

Fresh food: _____

Fresh food: _____

Protein: _____

Which foods probably have fat or oil in them?

_____ _____ _____

_____ _____ _____

Let's Find Out About You!

Go to a supermarket and look at the kinds of fruits and vegetables. Make a list of fruits and a list of vegetables. How many did you find there? Write their names here:

FRUITS	VEGETABLES
_____	_____
_____	_____
_____	_____
_____	_____
_____	_____

Which ones can you eat raw (without cooking)? Draw a * next to those foods. Which foods include a lot of oil or fat? Underline those foods. Draw a circle around your three favorite fruits and vegetables.

Step 14

Before You Read

1. What does the title "Practice Safety First" mean? Does the word *practice* in the title mean the same as in "Let's Practice"?
2. How do accidents happen?
3. Why do accidents happen? Is there always a human being as the reason? Why or why not?
4. What can a person do to help prevent accidents?

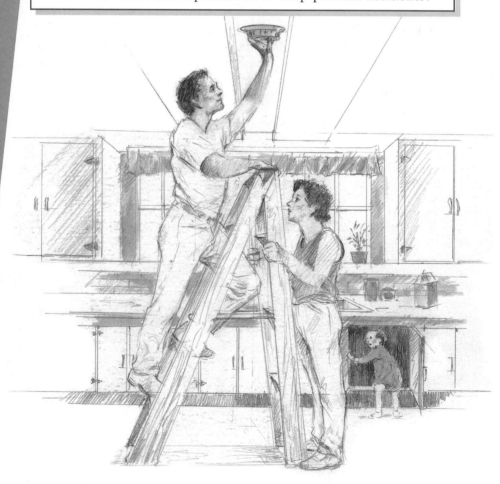

Practice Safety First

1   Accidents happen every day. We can't stop all accidents, but we can help prevent many of them. It helps us to know what causes most accidents. For example, most accidents happen to people in a hurry. Accidents sometimes happen
5   just because people do not think. They do not think about the dangers in some situations.

To help prevent accidents, we must learn to think of safety first. Here is one example:

A light bulb burns out, and a person needs to put in a
10   new light bulb. To do that, the person needs to reach up high. She could use an old chair to reach some high things. She could put the chair on a table. After all, a chair is easy to find fast. The chair may be handy, but is it safe? A person can easily fall from a chair. A chair is not the
15   right tool. It is not safe for climbing. A ladder is safe, but it takes time to get a ladder. It takes time to heal a broken leg too. To prevent accidents, people must learn to think before they do something dangerous! Accidents can hurt people. It is safe to use the right tool. Safety first really
20   saves time.

Are you a driver? Think about the dangers on roads too. Automobile accidents can kill. A car driver must always think about safety first. He must be alert. He must think about possible dangers on the road. For example, are
25   there wild animals in the forests? Might those animals run out into the road? Is the road wet and slippery? A person must think about possible dangers and be ready for them.

People can help their families prevent accidents. It's a good idea to read about safety and learn about ways to
30   be safe. It's a good idea to check one's houses for unsafe things. Stairs are especially dangerous. It is important to keep the steps clear. For example, can a person safely carry a box down the steps?

Most home accidents happen in the kitchen or bathroom.
35   People can burn themselves easily in the kitchen, and it is easy to fall on a wet floor. Bathrooms are dangerous because people fall in slippery bathtubs. There are other dangers, too. People should check their electrical equipment. A person who thinks of safety first is less likely to have an
40   accident.

We can't avoid all accidents, but we can all avoid some accidents. We can always think of safety before anything else. Safety first is a good saying. Safety first is a good habit, too. It saves time. It can save your life too.

≊ | Let's Learn from the Reading!

After you read the reading, answer these questions. You can also talk about them with the other people in your class.

1. Which of these causes accidents?
   a. hurrying
   b. thinking of safety first
   c. good habits

2. What is another reason for accidents?
   a. Someone checks the house for unsafe things.
   b. Someone is careless and doesn't think.
   c. Someone tries to help another person.

3. Why is the right tool best? (Circle all the right answers.)

   a. We can do a job safely with the right tool.

   b. We can avoid accidents.

   c. We can do the work in a short time.

4. How does the right tool save time? (Circle all the right answers.)

   a. Accidents don't just happen.

   b. We don't waste time with other tools.

   c. We can do the job safely and not get hurt.

   d. The wrong tool can cause damage.

5. Why must a driver think about safety first? (Circle all the right answers.)

   a. A person in a hurry might not drive safely.

   b. A driver must avoid accidents on hills.

   c. There are many possible dangers on the road.

6. Which sentence is like one in "Practice Safety First"? Find the sentence in the reading and underline it.

   a. It takes time to find a ladder.

   b. It also takes time to heal a broken leg.

   c. A person can easily fall from a chair.

7. What does *prevent* mean?

   a. avoid

   b. stop from happening

   c. think carefully

8. The title of this reading is "Practice Safety First." Which one of these other titles also fits the reading?

   a. Ladders and Tools

   b. Think About Safety

   c. Prevent Car Accidents

Let's Read More!

Is a Fire Really an Accident?

1   Accidents cause a lot of fires. Fires can burn people and destroy a lot of property too.

Many fires happen in factories. There are many things that are flammable (like chemicals and oils) in factories.
5   Flammable things can burn easily. Often there are NO SMOKING signs in parts of factories. Factory owners want to prevent fires.

Fires happen at home, too. Too much heat can cause fire. Therefore, heat is sometimes dangerous. Where is
10   there heat in a house? What are some dangerous things in a house? For example, kitchen stoves and furnaces are sometimes dangerous. If they are not clean, they can cause fires. If they do not work well, they can cause fires. Small heaters near curtains are very dangerous. Curtains
15   can catch on fire! Fires in fireplaces can sometimes be dangerous too.

Sometimes even people cause fires. It is hard to believe, but some people smoke in bed! They can fall asleep and start a fire. Children can cause fires too. Children find fires
20   interesting—and matches, too. They like to play with matches. If they light a match and their clothes catch on fire, they can get bad burns. The danger of matches is easy to understand.

Fires also happen outdoors. Every year there are forest
25   fires. Forest fires burn parks and valuable trees. There are also natural causes for fires. For example, lightning causes many fires, especially in forests. However, people's matches, cigarettes, and campfires also cause many of these fires.

30   The wind makes the fire spread over large areas. And it is
sad because many animals and trees die during a forest fire.

There is a good safety rule about matches: After you
use the match, blow it out. Then always break the match
into two pieces before you throw it away. If you can break
the match in your hand, the match is not hot. Cool matches
35   do not start fires.

Let's Learn from the Reading!

Here is a list of words you have seen so far in Steps 11–14. Use these
words in the answers to the questions.

gasoline	bathtubs	cloths	newspapers
tree	cigarettes	water	electricity
ladders	books	chair	food
signs	curtains	matches	heaters

1. Look at the list of materials. Which ones are flammable?

   _____

   _____

2. Which ones will not burn?

   _____

3. Some of these things will burn, but they will probably not start a
   fire. Which ones are they?

   _____

   _____

4. Think for a minute. What other things burn easily?

_____

_____

_____

5. How can cigarettes start a fire? (Circle all the right answers.)

   a. Cigarettes need matches to start burning. Matches are
      dangerous.

   b. If a person throws away a burning cigarette in a forest, it can
      burn dry leaves.

   c. People smoke a lot in their homes, and people can be careless.

   d. A smoker might fall asleep with a cigarette.

Let's Write!

There are some unsafe things in each of these pictures.
What's the danger here?

a. _____

   _____

   _____

   _____

   _____

b. _____

   _____

   _____

   _____

   _____

c. _____
   _____
   _____
   _____

d. _____
   _____
   _____
   _____

e. _____
   _____
   _____
   _____

f. _____
   _____
   _____
   _____

Let's Read More!

A Safe Home

1   Accidents happen everywhere. On the streets there are car accidents. In factories there are accidents with equipment. On farms there are accidents with machines. At home there are accidents too.

5   What causes accidents at home? There are three main causes: fire, falls, and poison. Fires cause many home injuries. Falls injure thousands of people. Poisons hurt many people too.

Where do accidents happen? There are four dangerous
10   places in a house. The kitchen is the most dangerous. The bathroom is also dangerous. Steps and chairs anywhere in the house are the third danger. The last dangerous area of a house is near the furnace.

A furnace is a large heater that keeps the house warm in
15   cold weather. In the winter, there is usually fire in a furnace. A clean furnace with a fire in it is safe. However, it must be clean. There must be a chimney for the smoke. The chimney must be clean too. Fires can start in dirty chimneys. Flammable things must not be near a hot furnace. Those
20   are the reasons for danger around furnaces.

Fires often happen in the kitchen. The stove is there for cooking. Sometimes food—like oil or fat—on the stove starts to burn. Oil on a hot stove can cause a big fire.

Electricity can cause fires too. Usually there is some
25   electrical equipment in a kitchen. So, there should be many separate outlets in the walls of a kitchen. Too many pieces of equipment can cause problems with the electricity, and that can start a fire. Check your kitchen for safety.

Are there many electrical cords to one outlet? Are all the
cords and wires in good condition?

Many people are hurt badly from falls. People often
climb on chairs so that they can reach up high. They can fall
easily from chairs. Falls often happen in the kitchen, too.
Sometimes food spills on the kitchen floor, and someone
can slip and fall on a wet and slippery floor.

The kitchen can be a dangerous place. Most people
have cleaning equipment in the kitchen. Cleaning liquids
are almost always poisons. Poisons can kill a person. It is
a good idea to store cleaning things in a safe place, out of
the reach of children. A high place can be safe—if children
can't climb up to it. A cupboard with a lock is a safe
place—if children cannot find the key.

Bathrooms are dangerous too. Bathtubs are slippery.
Many people fall and get hurt in bathtubs. Electricity in a
bathroom is dangerous too. A person can get a bad shock.
Keep electrical equipment far from water!

Steps and stairs are dangerous. Sometimes a person
cannot see small things on the steps. He or she could step
on these things, slip, and fall. Some people carry large and
heavy things up and down steps. This is dangerous too.
With many things in their hands, they cannot see the steps.

A home is not always dangerous. It can be a safe place.
But every member of the family must help. Everyone must
think about safety first.

Let's Learn from the Reading!

Let's answer these questions about the reading.

1. Where do most home accidents happen?

    a. in the bathroom

    b. in the kitchen

    c. on chairs and ladders

2. Why is food on the stove sometimes dangerous?

    _____

3. Sometimes food spills on the floor. Why is spilled food dangerous?

    a. It can burn and cause a fire.

    b. It can be slippery and cause a fall.

    c. It can be poison and make someone sick.

4. Why should a person put cleaning liquids in a safe place?

    a. They can burn and cause a fire in the kitchen.

    b. They are usually dangerous poisons.

    c. They cost a lot of money.

5. What is another possible title for the reading?

    a. Accidents on the Farm

    b. Four Dangerous Places in a Home

    c. Be Careful with Poisons!

6. Which sentence is in "A Safe Home"? Find the sentence in the reading and underline it.

    a. Most people have cleaning things in their kitchens.

    b. Cleaning liquids are almost always poisons.

    c. Therefore, a kitchen is a dangerous place.

7. Electrical cords for kitchen equipment fit into an outlet. Where is an electrical outlet?

    a. on the electrical equipment

    b. in the wall

    c. on the electrical cord

8. Explain the danger in the picture.

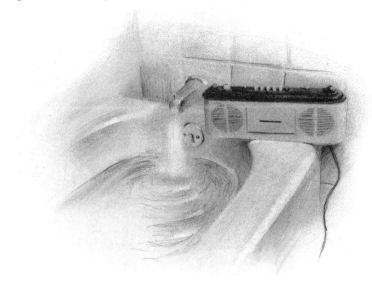

_____

_____

Let's Practice!

Here are several readings with more information for you. Read them.
Then do the exercises.

A. Poison. Be Careful!

Poisons are harmful to people because they can hurt or kill a person.
There are ways to prevent poisoning. There are ways to treat poisoning.
It is easier to prevent poisoning than to treat it.

In a home or an apartment, there are many chemicals. Look under a
kitchen sink. There is usually a liquid cleaner. Is it a poison? Is it
poisonous? Read the label. Here is an example:

> **CAUTION:** If swallowed, do not induce vomiting; this may
> be harmful. Keep out of eyes. If contact occurs, wash eyes
> immediately with water. Avoid contact with food. Rinse
> empty container with water before discarding.

Sometimes the instructions on labels are difficult to understand. What does this label mean? *Caution* is a warning to be careful. *To swallow* means "to drink." *To induce* means "to start" or "to cause." *Vomiting* means "losing the contents of the stomach through the mouth."

1. Read the first part of the label.

> **CAUTION:** If swallowed, do not induce vomiting; this may be harmful.

- Do not drink this liquid. If someone drinks some, do not let that person vomit. You can hurt yourself if you vomit.

2. Read the second warning on the label.

> Keep out of eyes. If contact occurs, wash eyes immediately with water.

- Keep this liquid away from eyes. *If contact occurs* means "if a person gets this liquid in his eyes."

Write the warning in other words. Use easier words.

_____

_____

_____

3. What does *Avoid contact with food* mean? Write the warning in easier words.

_____

_____

_____

4. Read these instructions from the label:

> Rinse empty container with water before discarding.

- *To rinse* means "to wash out with water." *Discarding* means "throwing away."

Use easier words to rewrite the label.

_____

_____

_____

B. Antidotes

One chemical in many kitchens and bathrooms is bleach. Bleach is useful for washing white clothes and cleaning things. Bleach makes things white again. It is useful, but it can be harmful. Look at the label on a bottle of bleach. Here is an example.

> CAUTION: USE ONLY AS DIRECTED.

- This sentence means "Be careful. Read all the instructions on the bottle. Follow them carefully."

Here are some more instructions on the bottle of bleach:

> INTERNAL: Feed lots of milk and then cooked cereal. Call a physician.
>
> IF SPLASHED IN EYES: Flush with water and call physician.
>
> EXTERNAL: Rinse immediately with water.

- An antidote is like medicine against poison.
- *Internal* means "inside the body."
  INTERNAL tells the antidote for bleach in the stomach.
- *External* means "outside the body."
  EXTERNAL tells the antidote for bleach on the skin.
- A physician is a doctor.

- *Splashed in eyes* means this: Some bleach touched the eyes or was near the eyes of the person.
- *Flush with water* means "wash out or rinse with a lot of water."

Now rewrite the instructions on the label in your own words.

_____

_____

_____

_____

People can prevent poisoning. Keep dangerous chemicals and medicines in safe places—out of the reach of children. Read the instructions on products and on medicines carefully. Throw away old medicine. Teach young people about the dangers of chemicals and medicines.

C. Category

Which word is not a part of the category? Find the different word and circle it. What is the category?

1.	stove	electricity	heater	furnace
2.	bleach	cleaner	poison	
3.	steps	kitchen	stairs	
4.	prevent	avoid	liquid	stop
5.	factory	farm	bathroom	
6.	kitchen	climb	bathroom	
7.	poison	spill	fall	fire
8.	bathtub	stove	furnace	heater
9.	paper	fire	matches	cloth
10.	doctor	farm	physician	
11.	alert	accident	awake	
12.	bathroom	ladder	stairs	

Let's Write!

Cause and Effect

How can we avoid accidents? And what are the effects of careful actions? Here are some sentences. In the first column, there are some ideas about carefulness. If you do these things, then you can help avoid an accident. In the second column are the results. Put these two ideas together. Write the number of the cause in front of the effect.

IF YOU...   THEN...

1. read labels on bottles   ____ you will not slip and
   carefully,   fall down.

2. put a rubber mat in   ____ children will not play
   a bathtub,   with them.

3. keep a light on over   ____ you can see and not
   stairs,   fall down.

4. keep pots and pans on   _1_ you will use the product
   the back of the stove,   carefully and safely.

5. keep matches in a   ____ you will be ready for
   safe place,   emergencies.

6. keep the number of the police,   ____ small children will not
   fire department, and hospital   pull them off and get
   help near your telephone,   burned.

Now rewrite all your sentences on these lines:

1. _____
   _____
   _____

2. _____
   _____
   _____

3. _____
   _____
   _____

4. _____
   _____
   _____

5. _____
   _____
   _____

6. _____
   _____
   _____

7. _____
   _____
   _____

Let's Find Out About You!

What safety checks do you need?

Look around your house or apartment. Is it safe? Here are some check lists. Then think about safety. Mark *YES* or *NO*. A *NO* answer shows danger.

SAFETY CHECKLIST

Safety Check Against Falls

	YES	NO
1. Does the bathtub have a rubber mat for safety?	☐	☐
2. Are steps clear?	☐	☐
3. Are small rugs safe from slipping?	☐	☐
4. Are stairs in good condition?	☐	☐
5. Do you use a strong ladder to climb to high places?	☐	☐
6. Is there enough light on stairs?	☐	☐

Safety Check Against Fire

	YES	NO
1. Are matches away from the stove and from heaters?	☐	☐
2. Is there a "No smoking in bed" rule?	☐	☐
3. Is your electrical system in good condition?	☐	☐
4. Is your heating system in good condition?	☐	☐
5. Does every person in your house know the emergency number?	☐	☐
6. Are clothes and curtains away from stoves and heaters?	☐	☐

Safety Check Against Poison

	YES	NO
1. Are all chemicals, cleaners, and medicines in safe places?	☐	☐
2. Can you read the labels on medicines and cleaning liquids?	☐	☐
3. Do you read labels on bottles carefully?	☐	☐
4. Do you follow instructions on medicines carefully?	☐	☐
5. Do you throw away old medicines?	☐	☐
6. Are the emergency numbers for doctors and the hospital near your telephone?	☐	☐

Step 15

Before You Read

1. What do you use for transportation?
2. Do you know how to drive?
3. Why do drivers need to pass a test to be able to drive a car on public roads?

Learn to Be a Good Driver

1   How can you learn to drive? There are many ways to learn to drive. One way is to ask a friend for help. If you do, look for a good driver to teach you. Ask your friend questions about driving. Are your friend's answers good?

5   Is your friend patient with you? Perhaps this friend will be able to teach you to be a good driver. Learning from another driver was the only way to learn to drive in the old days.

      Now, however, every driver must have a license. In fact,

10   a person even needs a driver's permit to learn to drive. Of course, laws about driving are not the same in all places. However, a student driver can go to a police station to find out about the laws. Most driving laws make sense because they make driving safe.

15   Now there are driving schools in most towns. The teachers (or driving instructors) learn special ways to teach. They have special equipment in their cars too. These special cars have dual controls. (*Dual* means "two.") Two sets of brakes make the car safer to drive. Both the student driver

20   and the instructor can use the brakes to stop the car. With dual brakes, the teacher can always control the car. For example, the teacher can halt (stop) the car to avoid danger.

      Driving schools put signs on their cars. These signs advertise the school. The signs also warn other drivers.

25   Sometimes the signs say STUDENT DRIVER. Most student drivers are very careful. However, they can make mistakes. In fact, any driver (or every driver) can cause an accident.

One little mistake in driving can put many other people in danger. On the road, a good driver sees the Student Driver

30   sign and watches a student-driver car carefully. In fact, a careful driver always pays attention to all other drivers.

Some secondary schools (like high schools) also teach driving. So, a lot of students take driving courses. They practice driving with their teacher. Furthermore, students

35   study driving rules in class. They learn the reasons for the rules, and they learn about road safety. They must understand the ideas behind safe driving and follow the rules. Drivers must learn to pay attention to many different things at one time. If all drivers follow the same rules,

40   then everyone is safer on the road.

Let's Learn from the Reading!

After you read the article, you should be able to answer these questions.

1. What kind of person is a good driving teacher? (Circle all the right answers.)
   a. someone who can drive a dual-control car
   b. a student driver
   c. a good driver and good teacher
   d. any patient person
   e. a person who can explain well

2. What equipment stops a car? _____

3. What does *dual* mean? _____

4. Describe a driving-school car. _____

   _____

   _____

5. It's a good idea for all drivers to watch student-driver cars. Why?

   a. The cars do not have brakes.

   b. The cars have dual controls.

   c. Student drivers are not careful.

   d. Student drivers make more mistakes than other drivers do.

6. What do students learn in driver's training courses? (Circle all the right answers.)

   a. how to avoid danger   d. where to drive

   b. to drive safely   e. how to stop a car safely

   c. about road safety   f. rules for driving a car on a public road

Let's Practice!

A. Look at the first picture.

1. What is the driver doing?

_____

2. Why is the other person in the car also paying attention?

_____

3. Is this car special in any way? How?

_____

B. Look at the second picture. This driver sees danger.

1. What is dangerous?

_____

_____

2. What can he do to avoid an accident?

_____

_____

3. Why is he a safe driver?

_____

_____

Let's Read More!

Drivers and Driving

1   Drivers do four things. They steer their cars. They make their cars go faster. They also slow their cars down. Every driver must also think about safety. It is part of the job. Safety depends on the answers to these four questions:

5   • How does the driver steer?

     • How fast does the driver go?

     • When and how does the driver slow down?

     • How much does the driver think about safety?

     Steering is the easiest part of driving. Beginning drivers

10   learn to steer without trouble. They also learn to control car speed, fast or slow. They only need practice.

     Thinking about safety is the hardest part of driving because beginning drivers do not know the dangers. They need practice in this area, too. They need to learn to

15   anticipate dangerous situations. *Anticipate* means "think about and expect."

     Here are some driving dangers to think about:

     1. Drivers in traffic are like a group of strangers. No driver knows the others. One driver can suddenly do

20   something dangerous, like change from one lane to another without warning or signaling. Good drivers watch other drivers and anticipate such surprises.

     2. Some places along roads are very dangerous. For example, there are many children near schools.

25   There are many pedestrians in busy cities. People who are walking on the streets may do something unusual, like change direction. A driver must be ready for anything and expect such things to happen.

3. Some parts of the road are dangerous. For example, hills and curves hide the roads. Trees and walls hide other cars. Bridges are often slippery.

4. Weather affects driving. Some people cannot see well in the rain. Snow and ice make slippery roads. In very hot weather, other drivers might be impatient, and that would affect their driving.

5. The roads are more dangerous at some times of the day. During the morning and evening hours, the sun shines in some drivers' eyes. Furthermore, rush hour is always a busy time on the roads. There are many cars on the road at rush hour. Many people are in a hurry then. At night, many drivers are tired, and perhaps some drivers are drunk.

Good drivers think about the situation. They expect surprises, and they always expect trouble. Other people's mistakes do not surprise them.

Let's Learn from the Reading!

Here are some questions about the reading. Can you answer them?

1. Safety depends on four things. What are they?

_____

_____

_____

_____

2. Which parts of driving are easy for beginning drivers? (Circle all the right answers.)

   a. starting the car

   b. anticipating danger

   c. steering the car

   d. going faster

   e. slowing the car down

   f. thinking about other drivers

3. Which of these ideas is hard to learn?

   a. starting the car

   b. anticipating danger

   c. steering the car

4. Why is it (the answer to number 3) hard to learn? (Circle all the right answers.)

   a. because people don't naturally do it

   b. because cars don't start easily

   c. because thinking ahead is not easy to learn

   d. because new drivers learn to steer the car

   e. because it is not easy to do many things at one time

5. What are some especially dangerous places along a road?

   _____

   _____

6. What happens during rush hour? When is it?

   a. People in cars hurry at the beginning and end of a work day.

   b. It is the time to go to movies or to restaurants.

   c. There is busy traffic late at night and on special days.

   d. The roads are busy from nine o'clock in the morning until three o'clock in the afternoon.

7. Why is rush hour a dangerous time?

   a. It often rains then.

   b. People in cars are hungry.

   c. There are too many cars on the road.

   d. Other drivers go too slow.

8. How can weather affect driving? (Circle all the right answers.)

   a. It can mean that the road is slippery.

   b. Rain usually hides some of the dangers on the road.

   c. Too many people are sleepy in bad weather.

   d. People are in a hurry and don't expect trouble on the road.

9. When is weather dangerous for driving? (Circle all the right answers.)

   a. when the road is icy

   b. when the sun shines in a driver's eyes

   c. when it's raining hard

   d. when it's raining and there are lots of children near the road

   e. during rush hour

   f. when the weather is hot

 Let's Read More!

Getting a Driver's License

1   Police officers sometimes stop drivers along the road. The first thing they ask is to see the driver's license. Every driver must have a license. It is a person's permission to drive. It also shows ability to drive and knowledge of the

5   rules.

      Secondary schools and driving schools teach driving. However, only governments give permission to drive. Each place (each country or state) has a special department for cars and for licenses. The name of this department is

10   different for each place, but they all do the same work. They give people licenses to drive.

A driver takes a test to get a license. Usually the test is in three parts. The first test is an eye test. Can the person see well enough to drive? The second part is a written test.

15   It is a test of rules. The questions are about the driving laws. The questions come from the driving rule book. Drivers study this book carefully before they take the test.

The third part of the test happens in the car. It is a road test, a test of driving ability. A testing official and the new

20   driver go for a ride. The official tells the driver to do certain things. For example, he or she tells the driver to park the car or to make a left turn. The driver must listen to the instructions and drive. The official watches for mistakes.

In some places, there are special roads for driving tests.

25   All the situations of driving are on these roads. The student driver must drive through the course to pass the test. Then the new driver can have a license to drive on public roads.

≋| **Let's Learn from the Reading!**

There are many ideas in the article. Here are some questions about those ideas. Can you answer them all? If you need to, read the article again.

1. What shows a person's driving ability?

   _____

   _____

2. Who gives licenses to new drivers?

   _____

3. What are the three parts of a driver's test?

_____

_____

_____

4. Why is the eye test so important?

_____

5. Explain the other two parts of the test. Why are they important?

_____

_____

_____

 Let's Talk!

Talk these questions over with one of your classmates.

1. What is name of the department for drivers' licenses in your area?
2. How much does a driver's license cost in your town?
3. How old must a person be to get a driver's license?
4. At what age should people stop driving?

 Let's Read More!

Road Signs

1   There are two kinds of road signs. Some have words on them, but others do not. Here are some common road signs.

You will notice that traffic signs have special shapes. Each shape is a different kind of sign. For example, all warning signs look like diamonds. All stop signs have eight sides. Railroad signs are circles. Upside-down triangles mean "yield." A yield sign is almost like a stop sign. At a yield sign, a driver must wait for drivers on the main street to pass. To *yield* means "to give up." On a sign, *yield* means "let other cars go first."

Stop signs are always red. The word STOP is usually on them. In some parts of the world, stop signs say "Halt!" These two words, *stop* and *halt*, mean the same thing. Yield signs are yellow. They sometimes have the word YIELD on them. Many warning signs are yellow. Most other signs are black and white. They tell about situations on the road. Some of these signs have words on them. Here are some more examples:

Along some roads, there are two kinds of traffic signs. There are signs with words. There are also international signs. All international signs are symbols, not words. The international signs are easy to understand. A person from any country can "read" international signs.

International signs show pictures of danger on the road ahead. Before a slippery bridge, there is a picture of a car slipping. It shows a car out of control.

Before a steep hill, there is a sign like this:
How steep is the hill? The percentage shows the

30   grade. A two percent (2%) grade means this:
The road gets 2 feet higher for every 100 feet of
distance.

Let's Write!

What do these other signs mean? Write the meaning in other words in
the blank.
Example:

means   *Do not drive into this road.*

1.   means _____

2.   _____

3.   _____

4.   _____

5.   _____

6.   _____

7.   _____

Let's Talk!

Talk with one or two of your classmates. Think about the signs along
the road. What are some other kinds of signs? What are the uses of
signs? Do we really need them? Why?

Let's Read More!

How Do Accidents Happen?

1   Sometimes a driver does not think about safety. There are sometimes other things on a driver's mind. These times are dangerous.

Some situations need special attention. Here are some

5   situations for you to think about. These are common causes of accidents:

1. Passing on a hill is dangerous. A third car on the other side of the hill can hit the passing car.

2. It is dangerous to be too close to the center line. A

10   driver should stay in the middle of a lane. It is necessary to have room to move—to avoid danger. For example, if the wind is strong, it can push a car into another lane. Or if a part of the road is bad, a driver could lose control.

15   3. High speed is always dangerous. A driver can lose control at fast speeds. Sometimes the road might be wet and slippery. Lower speeds are necessary then. Low speed is necessary on curves too.

4. Never race a train to a railroad crossing. Do not race

20   another car either. The roads are not for racing!

5. Do not pass another car at an intersection. There are usually a lot of cars at intersections. You cannot see all the cars.

6. Do not turn left at an intersection without stopping.

25   Watch for cars from all directions.

7. Be careful near pedestrians or bicyclists. People along the road can suddenly move into the road. Watch for children. Sometimes they suddenly go to the other side of the street.

30   8. Rushing is dangerous. Drivers in a hurry drive too
              fast. They go in front of other cars without warning.
              Sometimes they do not wait for traffic lights to
              change.

              Every driver must think about safety on the roads.
35   What is the answer to the problem of dangerous roads?
        Perhaps the answer is *courtesy*, which means "being polite."
        Each driver must be polite to other drivers. All drivers
        must follow the rules. Courtesy on the roads means safety
        for you and others.

Let's Learn from the Reading!

Read these questions and answer them. Then talk about your
answers with your classmates.

1. Why is speeding dangerous?

   a. Other drivers are too polite.

   b. Other drivers go too slow.

   c. It makes the road slippery.

   d. The driver cannot control the car.

2. When are roads slippery?

   a. in the morning

   b. after snow or rain has fallen

   c. in the sun

   d. when the wind blows hard

3. Why can a rushing driver have an accident?

   a. There isn't time to think and to stop.

   b. The car is moving too slow.

   c. The road is probably wet.

   d. There is too much snow.

Let's Talk!

With a classmate, talk over these questions.

1. In your part of the country, are there any special dangers for drivers? What are they?
2. When do most accidents happen?
3. If there is a car accident, what should a person do?

Let's Write!

Here are four accident reports. Talk about each situation with some classmates. What was the problem? What caused the accident?

1. The driver, a 32-year-old woman, hit a tree with her car. There was ice on the road. The driver was not hurt.

   _____

   _____

2. The driver, a 26-year-old male, drank six cans of beer at a party. He lost control of his car on an S-curve. The road was a dry road. It was 12:30 A.M. The car went down a 50-foot hill and hit a tree. The driver died. His passenger, a 23-year-old female, has a broken leg and face cuts. They were not wearing seat belts.

   _____

   _____

   _____

3. The driver, a 42-year-old male, left the highway and hit a telephone pole. It was 3:30 A.M. The driver started his trip at 11 A.M. He drove for sixteen hours. The driver has many injuries. He is in the hospital.

   _____

   _____

   _____

4 The driver, a 45-year-old female, left the right lane of the road. Her car crossed the center line. It hit a truck from the other direction. The accident happened at 5:30 P.M. The road was very wet. The driver was traveling at the speed limit. However, the tires of the vehicle were old. The driver died. The driver of the truck left the hospital after an hour. He was not hurt badly.

_____

_____

_____

Let's Practice!

Find Another Word

There is an underlined word or phrase in each of these sentences. Look in this lesson and find another word with a similar meaning. Write the sentence again, with the new word in the place of the underlined word. There are some clues to help you.

1. The car was on the wrong <u>side of the road</u>.

    The car was in the wrong _____ .

2. <u>The car and the truck</u> were not in good condition.

    The two _____ .

3. The driver did not know all the <u>laws</u> about driving.

    The driver didn't know all the driving _____ .

4. This car has <u>two</u> controls for the brakes.

    This car has _____ brakes.

5. That woman is waiting for her driver's <u>permit</u>.

    That woman is waiting for _____ .

6. A good driver <u>thinks about</u> dangers <u>and expects</u> such situations. (one word)

   A good driver _____ .

7. There are many <u>people who are walking</u> on city streets.

   There are many _____ .

8. Accidents happen at <u>turns in the road</u>.

   Accidents happen on _____ .

9. The <u>frozen water</u> on the road makes it dangerous.

   _____ .

10. Any <u>place where two roads come together</u> can be dangerous for pedestrians and drivers, too.

   _____ .

Let's Find Out About You!

Choose A or B.

A. Describe yourself as a driver.

B. How do you feel about driving?

_____

_____

_____

_____

_____

_____

_____

Plateau III
Money in the Bank

 Before You Read

Talk these ideas over with your classmates. What ideas do you expect to learn about in this part of the book ?

1. Look over the rest of this book. What do the pictures tell you?

   _____

   _____

2. Read the titles of the articles. What can you anticipate about the readings? What topics are likely?

   _____

   _____

   _____

   _____

3 Here is a list of words and phrases. Some of them may be new to you. Underline them. Then look at the other words. Will these words be important in this part of the book? Circle your answers.

money	banks	bathtubs	bills
electricity	saving money	gas	credit cards
vehicles	insurance	shopping	paper

Let's Go to the Bank!

1   Almost every town and every city has a bank. A bank is a building, and it is also a business. Banks are in the money business. Most intelligent people use banks for a number of reasons.

5   Every bank building is very strong. It must also be safe because the bank holds money for its customers. People take their money to the bank and deposit the money there. They want their money to be safe. The bank keeps money and other valuable items in a safe place. In fact, the name

10   of the special strong place for the money is "a safe." It is safe from fires and safe from thieves. (A thief takes money or things from their owners.)

     A bank is also a business. The bank uses people's money to make more money. The bank invests the money

15   in projects. *Invest* means "use money wisely to make more money." Invested money works to make more money.

Here is an example of invested money at work. Al and
Mira Gorski want to build a house, but they don't have
enough money. So they go to the bank and ask the bank
20   for a loan. A loan is money to use for a short time. Then
the Gorskis will have a place to live and they will pay back
the money. They will return it to the bank, part of the
amount each month. They also pay the bank some extra
money each month for the service. This extra money is
25   called "interest."

The Boggs family wants to start a business, so they go
to the bank for a loan too. Banks often lend money to
businesspeople. Like the Gorski family, the Boggs family
will use the money and pay it back, with interest. The
30   interest is part of the bank's profit—what the bank gets for
lending money.

The situation is simple: a bank lends the money. A
customer borrows it and uses it on a new project or on a
new business. So, the bank invests in a new house or a new
35   business. Each month, the borrower must pay back a part
of the money and the interest. The bank gets part of the
loan and the interest each month. That interest is a return
on the invested money. Interest is usually a percentage
(%) of the loan. If you have money in a bank, then that
40   bank is "your bank." Perhaps you need money for a project.
Then you can ask your bank for a loan. You might be able
to get a loan from your bank. If you have money in a bank,
your chances of getting a loan are greater.

Banks lend money and borrow it too. Some people
45   "lend" their money to their bank. For example, Maggie Barns
keeps her money in the bank. The bank pays Ms. Barns
interest on her money. The bank then lends Maggie's money
to people like the Gorskis and Boggses. In other words, the

Gorskis and the Boggses borrow from the bank. They pay

50   interest on their loans. The bank is in the middle, between

the lender and the borrower.

Lending and borrowing are a bank's business. A bank can lend and borrow money because of the interest. Getting interest is also part of the bank's business.

≈ | Let's Learn from the Reading!

What did you learn in the reading?

A. Borrow or Lend?

To borrow means "to get something (like money) from someone to use." *To lend* means "to give something (such as money) to someone to use." Which fits into these sentences?

1. Jon wants to buy a car. He goes to the bank. He needs to

    _____ some money. The bank can _____

    it to him.

2. Ted and Jim are at a store. Ted doesn't have much money with

    him. He _____ some from Jim. Jim _____

    some money to Ted. Ted will pay it back tomorrow.

3. People can borrow and lend other things, too.

    a. My car does not work. Can I _____ yours?

    b. Sometimes Jane needs a nice dress to wear for a party. Her sister has a lot of nice clothes. She has a lot of nice dresses.

        She _____ one to Jane.

    c. Can I _____ my pen to you? You need one.

    d. (At our neighbor's door…) Good morning, Ms. Jones. I am making a cake. I don't have any sugar. I'm sorry, but can I

        _____ some?

B. *True* or *False*?

Write *true* or *false* in each blank.

1. _____ A bank is a business.

2. _____ A bank has a safe for customers' money.

3. _____ All the customers' money always stays in the safe.

4. _____ Banks invest in many projects, like new businesses.

5. _____ *Interest* means the same as *invest*.

6. _____ Customers must give back the same amount of money as the loan from the bank.

 Let's Think Before We Read!

Use these questions to think about the next reading. What ideas do you anticipate?

1. Do you have money in your pocket? Is it paper money? There is another name for paper money: "bills." Any bill is an important piece of paper. Money is paper, and it is important. So, a name for one piece of paper money is a bill. How many bills do you have in your pocket?

2. Bills are something else, too. Every month you get a bill for telephone service. You get a gas bill, too. What other bills do you get?

3. Is your money metal money? One piece of metal money is a coin. What kind of money do you have? Is it bills? Or is it coins? Together paper money and coins are cash. How much cash do you have with you? Some people do not like to have much cash with them. They like to use checks or credit cards. Do you have a credit card?

Now Let's Read!

"Would You Like to Open a Checking Account?"

1   Bank customers get many services from banks. For example, banks keep money and other valuable things safe. Banks also give loans, pay interest, and offer checking accounts.

5   Perhaps you have money, and you want a safe place to keep it. Then you put your money into a bank. A lot of people like to keep most of their money in a bank. The bank uses that money. It invests the money. The customers get interest from the bank for that money. Their money

10   works for them at the bank. But the customers need to have money to pay for things every day. How can they have their money in the bank and also pay for things? Banks offer checking accounts for that purpose. A customer can open a checking account. The bank gives the customer a

15   checkbook. Then the person can use checks, not cash, to pay for purchases at stores.

     How does a checkbook work? A checkbook is a like a little notebook. On each "page" (check), there are places to write the date, the name of the store, and the dollar amount

20   of the check. The customer's name and checking account number are already printed on the check. In a store, this customer writes a check to pay for food or other items. The customer gives one check to the store. The store sends this check to the bank. The bank gives cash to the store for

25   the check. The bank takes the money from the customer's checking account at the bank.

At the end of the month, the bank sends the used checks to the customer. These checks then become "receipts." Such receipts are important because they prove payment of bills,
30   like your telephone bill.

Checking accounts are a safe and easy way to use money. Someone can take cash from you, but no one can use your checkbook. You can lose cash, but your money is usually safe in a checking account.

35   Banks also give good customers credit cards or debit cards. A credit card is like a short-term loan. At the end of the month, the customer must pay the bill. A debit card works like a check. Through a telephone connection, the
40   amount of money to pay a bill is withdrawn from the customer's account. These ways make spending money safer and more convenient.

 Let's Learn from the Reading!

Answer these questions about checks and checking accounts. Look at the reading again if you need to.

1. What must you write on a check? (Circle all the right answers.)
   a. the name of the store
   b. the date
   c. the amount of the check
   d. your account number
   e. your name
   f. what you purchase

2. What does a receipt do? (Circle all the right answers.)

    a. It helps you with your money.

    b. It proves payment of a bill.

    c. It uses money wisely.

    d. It opens a checking account for you.

3. Checkbooks are safe because... (Circle all the right answers.)

    a. no one can use your checks, only you.

    b. another person can have the same number.

    c. you can safely have a lot of money in your checking account.

    d. the bank keeps your checks for you.

4. What does the bank do with your money? (Circle all the right answers.)

    a. The bank uses your money to invest.

    b. It gives loans to people who need money.

    c. It gets interest with your money.

    d. It keeps your money in a safe.

5. Which sentence is like one in "Would You Like to Open a Checking Account?"? Find the sentence in the reading and circle it.

    a. The bank gives cash to the store for the check.

    b. You can lose coins, but your money is safe in a checking account.

    c. A person can take cash from you, but only you can use your checkbook.

    d. Receipts prove the payment of bills.

6. What is the main idea of this reading?

    a. Receipts are important records for a business.

    b. A bank pays interest on money in a checking account.

    c. Checking accounts are safe and easy to use.

    d. You need a checking account.

◆ | **Let's Read More!**

The ATM

1   Who works in a bank? There are many tellers, loan
officers, the bank manager, and department managers.
Usually, tellers talk with customers and help them. They
do a lot of the bank's business every day. Loan officers
5   work on lending money. New accounts managers help
people open checking or savings accounts.

Today's banks have one more worker, too. It is a quiet
worker. This worker does not go home to sleep. It does not
need to rest. It works all night long. It never talks, either.
10   What is the quiet banker? Can you guess? Of course, the
silent banker is a machine.

One of the common names for a banking machine is
"automated teller machine." Every automated teller machine
(or ATM) works alone, and it works after banking hours.
15   At night, a person can go to the ATM to get money.

Each banking machine is outside of the main part of the
bank. Or it may be in a special lobby, a room before the
main door. In some places, it may be on the outside wall of
the building. In most big cities, a customer uses a credit
20   card at a bank to get into the ATM room. The card opens
the door to the special lobby. The ATM may not be at the
bank at all. It could be in a supermarket, at a shopping
mall, or even in a hotel or gas station. There are ATMs in
airports and train stations. Most people do not like to carry
25   a lot of money, so ATMs are very popular.

Usually, ATMs at banks have bright lights around them
at night for safety. A customer uses a special credit card and
a number to get money from the machine. There is some

danger around automated teller machines. Someone might
30   see the customer at the ATM and then try to take the money.
It is a good idea to go to an ATM with another person. (Do
not go to an ATM alone if another person is just standing
near it!)

 ## Let's Learn from the Reading!

Try to answer these questions from the article.

1. What is a teller?
   a. a person
   b. a manager
   c. a machine
   d. a card

2. What does *silent* mean?
   a. bright
   b. special
   c. good
   d. quiet

3. "The automated teller machine is the silent banker." Which sentence or sentences explain this name?
   a. The automated teller machine does not talk.
   b. Most tellers are people, and they talk to customers.
   c. A customer does not talk with an automated teller machine.
   d. An automated teller machine makes a lot of noise.

Let's Practice!

Learn About United Bank

Read about the United Bank in the advertisement. Then read the questions about Mr. Porter and his business at the bank. Can you answer his questions?

UNITED BANK HOURS

918 W. Park Street

Main Office	8:30–5:30 Monday through Thursday
	8:30–7:00 Friday
	9:00–12:00 Saturday
Loan Office	10–3 Monday through Friday
	9–11 Saturday

Loans at the Main Office only!

Automated Teller Machine and Night Deposit Box
at main office and all branches

Branch offices at 2233 E. Hampton and 4545 S. Conway

Branch offices open 9–5, Monday through Friday

---

1. Mr. Porter wants to open a checking account at United Bank. Can he open an account on Saturday afternoon?   YES   NO

2. Can he put money into his account on Saturday afternoon?   YES   NO

3. Every Friday afternoon, Mr. Porter gets his paycheck. He leaves work at 5:00. Can he go into the bank after work on Friday?   YES   NO

4. Can he get $50 cash and put the rest in his checking account?   YES   NO

5. What does he use to put his money into the bank after bank hours?

   _____

6. Mr. Porter needs a loan. Where can he go for information?

   _____

7. What does Mr. Porter need to do to get money on Sunday?

_____

 Let's Read More!

A Savings Account

1   Most people save money because they want to have money for the future. Most people save their money in a bank. They open a savings account for their money. A bank is a safe place, and banks pay interest. Most banks
5   have insurance, too. Therefore, your money is always safe. No thief can steal the money from you.

There are different kinds of savings accounts at a bank. A smart customer puts money in several kinds of accounts. He or she goes to several banks and asks about the interest
10   rates, insurance, and other services. Then the intelligent saver chooses a bank.

A customer might have several accounts. In fact, most customers do. One account is a checking account. Another is a short-term (time) savings account. The third can be
15   a long-term (time) account. Some customers leave their money in the bank for a long time. They agree not to ask for the money. Usually banks pay higher interest on long-term accounts like these.

It is important to remember some things about banks:
20   • Banks are businesses. Their business is to invest money to get interest.
     • You can save your money in a bank. The bank, however, invests your money. It lends your money to others.
25   • Not all banks have insurance.

- Not all banks give customers the same services.
- It is a good idea to "shop around" for a good bank. Go to many banks and ask questions about their services. Then choose the bank that has the best service for you.

30

Why do you need a bank? Ask other people why they have a bank. Most people do a lot of business with their banks. For example, they keep their money safe in a bank. They use their checking accounts, and they often ask for loans. People frequently take out loans to buy cars. They also ask for loans for houses, furniture, doctor or hospital bills, and other needs. Banks want to lend money to people with a good credit history. If you borrow money and pay it back on time, then you will have a good credit history too.

35

Some people do not have good credit histories. Perhaps they didn't pay their loans on time. It is not easy for them to borrow money. Even if a customer has a bad checking account history, then he or she will have trouble getting a loan. It is also difficult to borrow money without a credit history. Some young people borrow money just to pay it back for the purpose of starting a credit history. With a good credit history, they will be able to borrow money for college or for a car.

40

45

Let's Practice!

Write *true* or *false* in each blank.

1. _____ Banks are in business to make money.

2. _____ Banks lend money to people with good credit histories.

3. _____ All banks give the same interest rates.

4. _____ Every bank has insurance to keep your money safe.

5. _____ Money in a long-term savings account stays there a long time.

6. _____ People with savings accounts can get loans from their bank.

7. _____ Some people borrow money for college from a bank.

8. _____ Most people have only savings accounts at banks.

 Let's Read More!

A Bank Works for Its Customers

1   A bank, as a business, wants to attract new customers, so banks advertise. They put advertisements in newspapers and on television. To get the attention of new customers, some banks offer free checking accounts. In other words,
5   it doesn't cost anything to have a checking account at those banks. Many customers come to those banks because they offer free accounts. Checking accounts are convenient and easy to use. Most banks, however, ask customers for a "service charge." The customers pay the service charge, a
10   certain amount of money, to use checks.

Another popular bank service is the use of automated teller machines. Bank customers can get money at any hour of the day or night. Banks advertise their ATMs. Therefore, they get new customers because people want
15   the convenience of an ATM.

Sometimes a person receives cash or checks from other people. Some banks give special envelopes to their customers. Then they can send checks from other people to the bank—and not have to go to the bank. It is not a
20   good idea, however, to send cash in the mail.

Another bank service is a night deposit box. A customer can put money in the bank after banking hours. She or he just puts it in the night deposit box.

Some banks have drive-up banking. There is a special
25 window on the side of the bank. A person in a vehicle does not need to get out to go into the building. She or he just drives up to the window and talks to a teller.

Banks usually also sell special checks. One kind is traveler's checks. You sign the check one time at the bank.
30 Then you must sign it another time to use it as cash when you spend it. You can use traveler's checks in most countries of the world. These checks are very useful. They make life easier and money safer for travelers.

Another kind of check is a cashier's check. This kind of
35 check has a guarantee on it. This check is not from a person, but from the bank. A cashier's check is always good.

Some bank customers sometimes do not use their checking accounts. Others don't have checking accounts. So, banks sell money orders to these people. A money
40 order is also a check from a bank. However, it is usually not for a large amount of money like a cashier's check.

Today, many banks also give credit cards to their customers. A credit card is a way of giving a loan to a customer. The customer must pay the money back to the
45 bank by the end of the month. If the customer does not pay the money to the bank on time, the bank gets interest. Interest on credit card loans is very high. Every month the bank sends a statement, a report, to the credit card customer. Most bank credit cards are also guarantee cards.
50 You write a check to a store, and then you show your bank card. The clerk in the store writes the number of your bank card on the check. It is a guarantee for the store.

There will be no problems with your check. The store will get the money from the bank.

55   Banks also have safe deposit boxes. Customers can put their valuable things in these boxes. Some valuable things are important papers, diamonds, gold, and very old things. Customers pay a small charge every month for the box in the safe at the bank.

60   One other service is called "direct deposit." Money from the customer's work can go directly to the bank. The bank can also pay the customer's normal bills. Normal bills are rent or house payments, gas bills, water bills, and electricity bills. Some customers have loans to pay too. A

65   bank will take the money to pay loans out of a customer's account too.

Banks want to keep their customers and get new ones. Therefore, they must give customers good service.

Let's Learn from the Reading!

What did you learn in the reading? These questions will check your understanding.

1. What do banks advertise?
   a. information about their safe
   b. news about the banking business
   c. their special services
   d. traveler's checks

2. Which ones are guaranteed checks? (Circle all the right answers.)
   a. a money order
   b. a cashier's check
   c. a traveler's check
   d. a personal check

3. Who can buy money orders from banks? (Circle all the right answers.)

  a. customers without checking accounts

  b. all customers with checking accounts

  c. direct deposit customers

  d. any person who wants to buy one

  e. restaurants and stores

4. Where can you keep your important papers?

  a. in your checking account

  b. in your savings account

  c. in a night deposit box

  d. in a safe deposit box

5. Why do banks give credit cards to good customers? (Circle all the right answers.)

  a. because it's a bank service

  b. to write checks

  c. to put money in a savings account

  d. because it tells the bank the person's name

  e. to get the high interest on credit-card loans

6. When do you need a cashier's check?

  a. when you need to send a guaranteed check of a large amount

  b. when you cannot put the money in an envelope and send it through the mail

  c. when you have no more checks left in your checkbook

  d. when you cannot buy a money order

7. Why is direct deposit popular? It is popular because…

  a. customers don't need to write checks to pay their bills.

  b. customers don't have to go to the bank with their checks from work.

  c. many customers go directly to the bank after work.

  d. many banks don't have night deposit boxes.

8. What are most customers' normal bills?

   a. restaurant bills

   b. doctor's bills and hospital bills

   c. house payments and bills for gas, water, and electricity

   d. store bills

 Let's Read More!

"But I Don't Like Banks!"

1   Some people are afraid of banks. But is that reasonable? Why are some people afraid of them? A bank is just a business. Just think about it.

Some bank buildings look very big and strong. Old
5   bank buildings have very few windows and very heavy doors. Many banks look cold, not like friendly places. New banks look friendly, of course, but some people still don't like banks.

Banks also use a lot of official papers. Some people are
10   not comfortable with a lot of forms. They do not like to fill out forms. Other people do not go to banks for another reason. They don't like the charges for services. They don't want to pay for a checking account. They use cash, not checks.

15   In some countries, people do not give their money to a stranger in a bank. They buy gold with their money. Gold is always valuable. These people wear their gold all the time. So, they always have the gold jewelry on them. They do not have to trust anyone. This way, their money
20   seems safer to them. What does a bank customer get? The bank customer has only a piece of paper, a receipt. That piece of paper means money in the bank. To some people, gold is better.

25 In fact, banks are very safe. You can trust a bank to keep your money safe. Most banks have insurance, so the customers cannot lose their money. If a thief comes in and takes the money from the bank, the insurance company pays the customer's money. So, the customer's money is safe in a bank.

30 A bank is safer in another way, too. A thief can get into a house more easily than a bank. A thief will take your valuable things. Every day someone loses all his money in an accidental fire. Every day someone loses her purse with a lot of money in it. Every day someone loses his money

35 to a thief. However, thieves cannot get other people's money from a bank easily. Banks give good service to their customers.

 Let's Practice!

Here are some exercises. You can practice with the ideas in this part of the book.

A. What Do You Know About Banks? Answer these questions.

1. It is safer to invest your money in a bank than in gold jewelry because... (Circle all the right answers.)

   a. there is insurance on money in the bank.

   b. a thief can steal gold jewelry.

   c. banks offer lots of services.

   d. you can always trust a bank.

2. Why are some people afraid of banks? (Circle all the right answers.)

   a. Some bank buildings look cold and unfriendly.

   b. They are afraid of official papers.

   c. They don't trust strangers.

   d. There are thieves in banks.

3. Bank insurance is important to a customer because...

    a. someone checks on banks with insurance.

    b. customers cannot lose their money in a bank with insurance.

    c. banks with insurance pay more interest.

    d. you can lose your money or your purse to a thief.

4. Some people invest in jewelry because...

    a. gold is always valuable.

    b. they want to have their money with them.

    c. they don't trust the strangers in banks.

    d. (All these answers are right.)

B. Category

Which word is not a part of the category? Find the different word and circle it. What is the category?

1. money	bank	building	
2. save	lend	borrow	
3. cash	check	money	bills
4. customers	bank	people	
5. dollars	bills	coins	
6. money order	cashier's check	traveler's check	
7. buy	save	invest	
8. borrow	lend	interest	
9. deposit	teller	manager	
10. spend	save	keep	
11. say	hear	tell	
12. teller	receipt	check	
13. customer	bank	store	
14. interest	charge	trust	
15. teller	loan officer	customer	bank manager

Let's Talk!

Talk about these questions and your answers with a classmate.

1. How do you feel about banks?
2. Do you have an account at a bank? (What kind?)
3. What do you think? Is this sentence true or false? "My money is safer in a box under my bed than in a bank."

 ## Let's Write!

Mrs. Conrad goes the bank. She wants to open a new account. Can you help her?
Fill in the blanks. Read the next line for help from the teller!

(At the bank, at the new accounts desk ...)

Teller:	How can I help you?
Mrs. Conrad:	_____
Teller:	How much money do you want to deposit?
Mrs. Conrad:	_____
Teller:	Which kind of checks do you want? The plain ones? The ones with the blue sky and white clouds? Or the ones with flowers?
Mrs. Conrad:	_____
Teller:	Do you want your name and address on your checks?
Mrs. Conrad:	_____
Teller:	No, Mrs. Conrad. The charge is the same.
Mrs. Conrad:	_____
Teller:	Thank you. You will have your checks in a few days.

Let's Write!

Your aunt and uncle have sent you some money. You need to write them a thank-you letter. Here are some sentences from such a letter. Put them in a natural order. Then rewrite the letter. You can add other sentences. You can change the sentences too.

_____   Shall I come to visit you at that time?

_____   Thank you very much for the gift.

_____   I hope that you are well and happy.

_____   My plane will stop at the airport near you.

_____   Please excuse me for not writing sooner.

_____   I would like to see you.

_____   It's a long time since I last saw you.

_____   Dear Aunt Mary and Uncle Ted,

_____   Next month I plan to fly home.

_____   You are very kind people.

_____   Thanks again.

_____   I want to thank you in person.

_____

_____

_____

_____

_____

_____

_____

_____

_____

_____

Let's Find Out About You!

You have a wonderful gift from your aunt and uncle. It is $500. What will you do with it? Read the list below. Which one is the most important to you? Write "1" next to the most important one. Write "2" next to the second most important. Number the other three in order of importance.

There are no right answers, but you can learn something about yourself. Then think for a minute. Is there something else you want to spend money on?

_____	Pay all my bills.
_____	Buy some new clothes.
_____	Put the money in my savings account.
_____	Take a vacation.
_____	Buy a car.
_____	_____

Word List

Word List

Steps and Plateaus is built around a basic vocabulary of about 500 words. The basic words are introduced early in the text and are recycled throughout the Steps and Plateaus. In addition, approximately 750 additional vocabulary words of common usage and high frequency are introduced in context within the text. Some proper nouns are not included in this Word List.

For each word that is entered in the list, the following information is provided:

- the part of speech
- the number of the Step (1–15) or Plateau (I, II, or III) in which the word first occurs

Annotations

n	→	noun
n pl	→	plural noun
v	→	verb
modal v	→	modal verb
v past	→	irregular past tense form
pron	→	pronoun
adj	→	adjective
adv	→	adverb
prep	→	preposition
int	→	interjection
conj	→	conjunction
idiom	→	idiom

A

a (adj) 1
ability (n) 15
able (adj) 7
about (prep) 1
above (prep) I
accident (n) 9
according (prep) II
account (n) III
ache (n) 8
across (prep) I
action (n) 12
add (v) I
address (n) 1
advertise (v) II
advertisement (n) 11
advertising (n) 10
advice (n) 8
Aesop (n) 7
afford (v) II
afraid (adj) 7
Africa (n) I
after (prep, conj) 1, 13
afternoon (n) 4
again (adv) I
against (prep) 9
age (n) 15
ago (adv) 4
agree (v) I
ahead (adv) 15
air (n) I
airport (n) III
alarm (n) 12
alert (adj) 14
alike (adj) 7
all (adj) 1
almost (adv) 3
alone (adj) I
along (adv) 15
already (adv) 10
also (adv) 2
always (adv) 5

am (v) 1
amount (n) 11
an (adj) 1
and (conj) 1
animal (n) 1
another (n, adj) 1, 3
answer (n, v) 2
Antarctica (n) I
anticipate (v) 15
any (adj) 7
anymore (adv) 6
anything (pron) 4
anyway (adv) 7
anywhere (adv) 12
apartment (n) 6
apple (n) 8
April (n) 4
are (v) 1
area (n) I
aren't (v) I
around (prep) 1
arrive (v) 6
art (n) 2
article (n) 3
as (conj) 5
Asia (n) 5
ask (v) 1
at (prep) 1
at all (idiom) 7
attention (n) 15
attract (v) III
August (n) 4
aunt (n) III
Australia (n) I
average (adj) II
avoid (v) 12
away (adv) 6

B

baby (n) 1
back (adv, n) 2, 8
backache (n) 8

bad (adj) I
badly (adv) 14
bag (n) 11
balanced (adj) 13
ball (n) I
banana (n) 13
bank (n) III
banker (n) III
barn (n) 9
basic (adj) II
bathroom (n) 14
bathtub (n) 14
be (v) 1
beach (n) 10
beans (n pl) 13
bear (n) 7
beautiful (adj) 1
became (v past) 7
because (conj) 1
become (v) 9
bed (n) 9
bedroom (n) 12
bee (n) 9
beef (n) 11
beer (n) 15
before (prep) 1
began (v past) 5
begin (v) 1
behind (prep) 7
bell (n) 4
belong (v) 10
belt (n) 15
best (adv, adj) I, 11
better (adv, adj) 3, 9
between (prep) 1
bicycle (n) 5
bicyclist (n) 15
big (adj) 1
bill (n) III
bird (n) 4
birthday (n) I
bit (n) 7

black (adj) 4
blackboard (n) 4
blank (n) 2
blanket (n) 9
bleach (n) II
blond (adj) I
blouse (n) II
blue (adj) 5
board (n) II
boat (n) I
body (n) I
book (n) 1
border (n) I
(be) born (v) 4
borrow (v) III
borrower (n) III
both (adj) I
bottle (n) 8
box (n) 9
boy (n) 1
brakes (n pl) 15
brand (n) II
bread (n) 7
breakfast (n) 9
breathe (v) I
bridge (n) 15
bright (adj) 3
bring (v) 2
broken (adj) 10
brother (n) 1
budget (n) 11
build (v) 9
building (n) 1
built (v past) 9
bulb (n) 14
bulk (n) 11
burn (v, n) 12, 14
bus (n) 5
business (n) 5
businessman (n) II
businesspeople (n) 5
busy (adj) 6

but (conj) 2
button (n) II
buy (v, n) 3, 11
by (prep) 3

C

cake (n) 13
calendar (n) 4
call (v) 2
(be) called (v) 8
came (v past) 7
can (modal v) 1
can (n) 10
can't (modal v) 3
candy (n) 8
cannot (modal v) 3
cape (n) II
car (n) 2
carbohydrate (n) 13
card (n) 6
care (n, v) I, 10
career (n) 3
careful (adj) 10
carefully (adv) 8
carefulness (n) 14
careless (adj) 14
carrot (n) 13
carry (v) 8
cash (n) III
cat (n) 1
catalog (n) II
category (n) II
cause (v, n) 12
cave (n) II
celery (n) 13
Celsius (n) 8
center (adj) 15
centimeter (n) II
cereal (n) 13
certain (adj) 15
chair (n) 2
change (v, n) 4, 5

charge (n) III
chart (n) II
cheap (adj) 4
cheaply (adv) 11
check (v, n) 8, 14
checkbook (n) III
checking (adj) III
cheese (n) 11
chemical (n) 12
chest (n) II
chicken (n) 7
child/children (n/n pl) 1
chimney (n) 14
chips (n pl) 13
choose (v) 10
Christian (adj) I
church (n) 5
churchmen (n pl) 5
cigarette (n) 10
circle (n, v) 1, 2
city (n) 1
class (n) 1
classmate (n) 5
classroom (n) 1
clean (v, adj) 9, 10
cleaner (n) 14
clear (adj) 12
clever (adj) 7
climate (n) I
climb (v) 14
clock (n) 4
close (v, adj) 2, 12
closet (n) II
cloth (n) 9
clothes (n pl) 3
clothing (n) II
cloud (n) III
club (n) 6
coal (n) I
coat (n) II
coin (n) III
cold (adj, n) I

collect (v) 12
college (n) 6
color (n) I
colorfast (adj) II
colorful (adj) 3
column (n) 14
combination (n) II
come (v) 1
comfortable (adj) II
common (adj) II
compare (v) II
complete (v) 2
computer (n) 2
condition (n) 14
contact (n) 14
contain (v) 12
continent (n) I
control (n, v) 15
convenience (n) 11
convenient (adj) III
cook (v) 9
cookie (n) 13
cool (adj) II
co-op (n) 9
cooperate (v) 9
cooperation (n) 9
cooperative (n, adj) 9
cord (n) 14
corn (n) 13
corner (n) 2
correct (adj) 2
cosmetics (n pl) 8
cost (v, n) 4, I
cotton (n) II
could (modal v) 5
country (n) 1
course (n) 1
courtesy (n) 15
cover (v, n) I
credit (n) III
credit card (n) III
crop (n) 5

cross (v) 15
crow (n) 7
crowd (n) 6
cry (v) 7
culture (n) I
cup (n) 13
cupboard (n) 11
curly (adj) I
curtains (n pl) 12
curve (n) 15
custom (n) I
customer (n) 11
cut (v, n) II, 15
cycle (n) II

D

damage (n) 12
dance (v) 6
danger (n) 12
dangerous (adj) 8
dark (adj) I
date (n) 5
daughter (n) 1
day (n) 1
dear (adj) 1
December (n) 4
decorations (n pl) II
degree (n) 8
dentist (n) 3
department (n) II
deposit (n, v) III
describe (v) I
desk (n) 4
dessert (n) 13
destroy (v) 12
detector (n) 12
diamond (n) 5
dictionary (n) 2
did/didn't (v past) 4
die (v) 12
diet (n) 13
difference (n) I

different (adj) I
difficult (adj) 9
dinner (n) 9
direct (adj, v) III, 8
direction (n) 8
directions (n pl) I
dirty (adj) 9
disaster (n) 12
discard (v) 14
discount (n) II
distance (n) 15
do/does (v) 1
doctor (n) 3
dog (n) 1
dollar (n) II
don't (v) 1
door (n) 2
down (adv) 7
dozen (n) 11
drank (v past) 15
draw (v) 1
dress (n) II
drill (n) 12
drink (v, n) I, 8
drip-dry (v) II
drive (v) 5
driver (n) 5
driving (n) 15
drop (v) 7
drove (v past) 15
drugstore (n) 8
drunk (adj) 15
dry (adj) I
dry cleaning (n) II
dryer (n) II
dual (adj) 15
duck (n) 7

E

each (adj, pron) 1, I
ear (n) 8
earache (n) 8

early (adj) 9
earn (v) I
Earth (n) 5
earthquake (n) I
easier (adj) 4
easily (adv) 3
east (n, adj) I
easy (adj) 3
eat (v) I
effect (n) 14
egg (n) 7
eight (adj) 2
eighteen (adj) 2
eighth (adj) 4
eighty (adj) 3
either (adj, adv) 4
electrical (adj) 12
electricity (n) 12
eleven (adj) 2
eleventh (adj) 4
emergency (n, adj) 9, 12
empty (adj) 10
end (n, v) 1, I
energy (n) 13
English (n) 1
English-speaking (adj) 5
enjoy (v) 1
enough (adv) 7
envelope (n) 1
equal (v) 3
equipment (n) 12
escape (v) 12
Eskimo (n) I
especially (adv) 12
Europe (n) 5
even (adv) 1
evening (n) 4
ever (adv) 6
every (adj) 1
everybody (pron) I
everyone (pron) 2
everything (pron) 4

everywhere (adv) 4
example (n) 1
excuse (n) III
exercise (n) 1
expect (v) 12
expensive (adj) 4
explain (v) 7
extinguisher (n) 12
extra (adj) II
eye (n) I

F

fable (n) 7
face (n) 5
fact (n) 1
factory (n) 14
fade (v) II
Fahrenheit (n) 8
fall (n, v) 5, 7
false (adj) 1
familiar (adj) 7
family (n) 1
famous (adj) 4
far (adv) I
farm (n) 3
farmer (n) 3
farming (adj, n) 3, 5
fashion (n) II
fast (adv) 2
fat (n) 11
father (n) 1
favorite (adj) 11
feather (n) 4
February (n) 4
feel (v) 5
feet (n pl) II
fell (v past) 7
female (n) 15
fence (n) 9
fever (n) 8
few (adj) 5
fiber (n) II

field (n) 5
fifteen (adj) 2
fifth (adj) 4
fifty (adj) 3
fill (v) 1
find (v) 1
fine (adj) 7
fire (n) 12
fire department (n) 12
fire drill (n) 12
fireplace (n) 12
first (adj) 1
fish (n) I
fit (v) I
five (adj) 2
fix (v) 9
flammable (adj) 12
flax (n) II
float (v) 7
floor (n) 12
flower (n) 5
fly (v) III
follow (v) 1
following (adj) II
food (n) 3
foot (n) 8
for (prep) 1
forest (n) 7
forget (v) 12
formal (adj) II
forty (adj) 3
four (adj) 2
fourteen (adj) 2
fourth (adj) 4
fox (n) 7
free (adj) I
freezer (n) 11
frequently (adv) III
fresh (adj) I
Friday (n) 4
friend (n) 1
friendly (adj) 6

from (prep) 1
front (n) 2
frozen (adj) 11
fruit (n) 11
fuel (n) 12
full (adj) 5
fun (n) 2
funny (adj) 5
fur (n) II
furnace (n) 12
furniture (n) III
furthermore (adv) 13
future (n) III

G

game (n) I
garbage (n) 10
garden (n) I
gas (n) 12
gather (v) 9
gave (v past) 4
gentle (adj) II
geographer (n) I
geography (n) I
get (v) 3
gift (n) 7
girl (n) 1
give (v) 1
glad (adj) 1
globe (n) I
go (v) 2
gold (n, adj) 7
golden (adj) 7
golf (n) 3
good (adj, n) 2, 7
good-bye (int) 1
goose (n) 7
government (n) 15
grade (n) 11
grain (n) 11
gram (n) 11
grandfather (n) 1

grandmother (n) 1
great (adj) I
greedy (adj) 7
green (adj) 5
grew (v past) 5
ground (n) I
group (n) 1
grow (v) 5
guarantee (n) III
guess (v) I

H

habit (n) 13
had (v past) 1
hair (n) I
half (n) I
hall (n) 6
halt (v) 15
hand (n) 8
handy (adj) 14
happen (v) 5
happy (adj) 2
hard (adv) 4
harmful (adj) 13
harvest (n) 5
has/have (v) 1
he (pron) 1
head (n) 7
headache (n) 8
heal (v) 14
health (n) I
healthful (adj) 13
healthy (adj) I
hear (v) 7
heart (n) 5
heat (n) 12
heater (n) 12
heavy (adj) 14
height (n) II
hello (int) 1
help (v, n) 1, 3
her (adj, pron) 1, 6

here (adv) 1
hers (pron) II
hide (v) 12
high (adj, adv) I
highway (n) 15
hill (n) 14
him (pron) 2
hip (n) II
his (pron, adj) 1, 12
historian (n) II
history (n) 2
hit (v) 7
hold (v) 12
holiday (n) 5
home (n) 3
homeless (adj) 6
hometown (n) 13
hope (v) III
hospital (n) 3
hot (adj) I
hour (n) 5
house (n) 1
how (adv) 1
however (adv) 5
human being (n) I
hundred (adj) 2
hungry (adj) 6
hunt (v) I
hurry (n, v) 8, 15
hurt (adj, v) 6, I
husband (n) 1
husky (adj) II

I

I (prep) 1
ice (n) I
ice cream (n) 8
icy (adj) 15
idea (n) 1
if (conj) 1
immediately (adv) 14
impatient (adj) 15

importance (n) 13
important (adj) 1
in (prep) 1
inch (n) II
include (v) II
induce (v) 14
information (n) 1
ingredient (n) 13
injure (v) 14
injury (n) 14
ink (n) 4
inside (prep, n) 7, II
instructions (n pl) II
instructor (n) 15
insurance (n) III
intelligent (adj) 7
interest (n) III
interesting (adj) 1
international (adj) 15
intersection (n) 15
into (prep) I
introduce (v) 1
invest (v) III
invite (v) 9
iron (n) II
ironing (n) II
is (v) 1
island (n) I
it (pron) 1
item (n) 2

J

jacket (n) II
January (n) 4
job (n) I
join (v) 9
journal (n) 3
juice (n) 11
July (n) 4
June (n) 4
junior (adj) 1
junk (n) 13

just (adv) 3

K

keep/kept (v/v past) 3/5
key (n) 14
kill (v) 7
kilogram (n) 11
kind (n) 2
king (n) 5
kitchen (n) 6
knew (v past) 5
knife (n) 5
know/knew (v/v past) 2/5

L

label (n) 8
ladder (n) 12
lake (n) I
land (n) I
land mass (n) I
lane (n) 15
language (n) I
large (adj) 2
last (adj, v) 1, II
late (adv) 4
latest (adj) 3
law (n) II
lawyer (n) 3
lay (v) 7
leaves (n pl) II
Leap Year (n) 5
learn (v) 1
leather (n) II
leave/left (v/v past) 4
left (adj) 11
left turn (n) 15
leg (n) 14
lend (v) III
lender (n) III
less (adv) 9
lesson (n) 2
let/let's (v) 1

letter (n) 1
level (n) 13
librarian (n) 2
library (n) 2
license (n) 15
life (n) 2
life-giver (n) I
lifestyle (n) II
light (n, adj) 5, I
light bulb (n) 14
like (prep, v) 1
likely (adj) 14
limit (n) 15
line (n) 1
lipstick (n) 8
liquid (n, adj) I
list (n, v) 2
listen (v) 4
literature (n) 2
litter (n) 10
litterbug (n) 10
little (adj) 1
live (v) 1
living room (n) 12
loaf (n) 11
loan (n) III
lobby (n) III
lock (n) 14
lonely (adj) 6
long (adj) 5
look (v) 1
lose (v) 11
lot (n) 1
lots (n pl) 2
loud (adv, adj) 2, 7
low (adj) II
low-fat (adj) 11
lunch (n) 7

M

machine (n) 9
made (v past) 5

magazine (n) 2
maiden name (n) 1
mail (n) 1
main (adj) 1
make (v) 3
make-up (n) 8
male (n) 15
mall (n) III
man (n) 1
manager (n) III
manufactured (adj) 13
many (adj) 1
map (n) 2
March (n) 4
margarine (n) 13
mark (n, v) 5
marriage (n) 1
married (v, adj) 1
mass (n) I
mat (n) 14
match (v) II
matches (n pl) 12
material (n) II
matter (v) 10
May (n) 4
maybe (adv) 6
me (pron) 1
meal (n) 8
mean (v) 1
meaning (n) 1
meant (v past) 5
measure (v, n) 5
measurement (n) II
meat (n) I
medicine (n) 3
medium (adj) II
meet (v) 1
member (n) 9
men (n pl) 1
menu (n) 11
metal (n) I
mice (n pl) 7

middle (adj, n) 1, I
might (modal v) 12
mild (adj) II
mile (n) 6
milk (n) 7
million (n, adj) 3
mind (v) I
mine (pron) 1
minerals (n pl) 13
minus (prep) 3
minute (n) 5
Miss (n) 1
mistake (n) 5
mix (v) II
moan (v) 7
modern (adj) I
Monday (n) 4
money (n) 4
month (n) 1
moon (n) 5
moral (n) 7
more (adv) 1
morning (n) 4
mosque (n) 6
most (adj) 1
mostly (adv) I
mother (n) 1
mountain (n) I
mouse (n) 7
mouth (n) 7
move (v) I
Mr. (n) 1
Mrs. (n) 1
Ms. (n) 1
much (adv) 1
mulberry (n) II
muscle (n) 13
museum (n) 10
Muslim (adj, n) 4, I
must (modal v) 2
my (adj) 1
myself (pron) 1

N

name (n) 1
natural (adj) I
naturally (adv) 12
near (prep) 2
nearby (adv) 6
necessary (adj) 4
need (v) 1
neighbor (n) 6
new (adj) 2
news (adj, n) 3
newspaper (n) 2
next (adj) 5
nice (adj) 1
night (n) 2
nine (adj) 2
nineteen (adj) 2
ninety (adj) 3
ninety-eight point six
   (adj) 8
ninth (adj) 4
no (adj, int) 4
noise (n) 7
noon (n) 9
normal (adj) 8
north (n, adj) I
North America (n) 4
North Pole (n) I
northern (adj) I
nose (n) 8
not (adv) 1
notebook (n) 4
notes (n) 4
nothing (pron) 7
November (n) 4
now (adv) 1
number (n) 1
nut (n) 7
nutrition (n) 11
nutritious (adj) 13

O

occur (v) 14
ocean (n) I
October (n) 4
of (prep) 1
of course (idiom) 1
off (adv) 8
office (n) III
officer (n) 15
often (adv) 4
oil (n) I
oily (adj) 12
okay (int) 2
old (adj) 1
on (prep) 1
once (adv) 5
one (adj, pron) 1, 2
only (adv) 1
open (v, adj) 2, I
opposite (n) 10
or (conj) 1
orange (n) 13
order (v) II
organization (n) 9
other (n, adj) 1
ounce (n) 11
our (pron, adj) I
ourselves (pron) 9
out (adv) 12
outlet (n) 14
outside (n, adv) II, 12
over (adv) 12
own (adj, v) 3, 7
owner (n) 14
oxygen (n) 12

P

package (n) 11
page (n) 10
pain (n) 8
pair (n) 10
pan (n) 14

pants (n pl) II
paper (n) 1
paragraph (n) 5
parent (n) 6
park (n, v) 10, 15
part (n) 1
party (n) 9
pass (v) 15
passenger (n) 15
pasta (n) 13
patient (n, adj) 8, 15
pattern (n) 5
pay (v) I
pay attention to (idiom) 15
paycheck (n) III
payment (n) II
peace (n) I
peanut (n) 13
pedestrian (n) 15
pen (n) 4
pencil (n) 1
people (n pl) 1
percent (n) I
percentage (n) II
perhaps (adv) I
permanent press (adj) II
permission (n) 15
permit (n) 15
person (n) 1
pharmacist (n) 3
philosophy (n) 2
phrase (n) 1
picnic (n) 10
picture (n) 2
pie (n) 13
piece (n) I
pile (n) 12
pill (n) 8
pizza (n) 11
place (n) 1
plain (adj) III
plan (v, n) 8, II

plane (n) III
planet (n) I
plant (n, v) 5
plate (n) I
plateau (n) I
play (v) 2
player (n) 6
please (int) 1
plus (prep) 3
pocket (n) III
poison (n) 14
pole (n) 15
police (n) 10
polite (adj) 15
pollution (n) 10
poor (adj) II
popcorn (n) 13
popular (adj) 3
possible (adj) 11
post office (n) 1
postal code (n) 1
pot (n) 14
potato (n) 13
pound (n) 11
powder (n) 8
practice (v, n) 1
prepare (v) 9
prescription (n) 8
pretty (adj) 7
prevent (v) 12
price (n) II
probably (adv) 10
problem (n) 7
produce (n) 11
product (n) I
profession (n) 3
professional (n, adj) 3
program (n) 2
project (n) III
protein (n) 13
prove (v) III
proverb (n) 7

public (adj) 2
pull (v) 14
purchase (n) III
purpose (n) III
push (v) 15
put (v) 1
pyramid (n) 13

Q

quality (n) II
question (n) 1
quickly (adv) I
quiet (adj) 2
quilt (n) 9

R

race (v) 15
radio (n) 10
rag (n) 12
railroad (n) 15
rain (n) I
ran (v past) 7
rang (v past) 4
rate (n) III
raw (adj) 13
reach (n, v) 8, 14
read (v) 1
reading (n) 1
ready (adj) 9
ready-made (adj) II
ready-to-wear (adj) II
real (adj) 5
really (adv) 4
reason (n) 5
reasonable (adj) III
receipt (n) II
records (n pl) 5
red (adj) 5
refined (adj) 13
refrigerator (n) 11
religion (n) I
remember (v) 5

remove (v) II
report (n) 12
resource (n) I
rest (n) 12
result (n) 9
return (n) III
rewrite (v) 14
rice (n) II
rich (adj) 5
ride (v, n) 5, 15
right (adj) 1
rinse (v) 14
rise (v) 12
river (n) 1
road (n) 5
rock (n) I
roll (v) 12
Roman (adj) 5
room (n) 2
rubber (n) 14
rug (n) 12
ruin (v) II
rule (n) 11
run (v) 12
rush (adj, v) 15
rush hour (n) 15

S

safe (adj, n) I, III
safely (adv) 12
safety (n) 12
said (v past) 7
sale (n) 8
salt (n) I
same (adj) 1
sand (n) 10
sang (v past) 7
sat (v past) 4
Saturday (n) 4
save (v) 9
savings (n pl) III
saw (v past) 7

say (v) 2
saying (n) 7
school (n) 1
sea (n) I
seamstress (n) II
season (n) 5
seat belt (n) 15
second (adj, n) 4, 5
second-hand (adj) II
secondary (adj) 15
see (v) 5
seem (v) 5
seldom (adv) 11
sell (v) 3
seller (n) 5
send (v) III
senior (adj) 1
sent (v past) 1
sentence (n) 1
separate (adj) I
September (n) 1
serious (adj) 10
service (n) III
serving (n) 13
set (n) 15
setting (n) II
seven (adj) 2
seventeen (adj) 2
seventh (adj) 4
seventy (adj) 3
several (adj) 7
sew (v) II
sewing (n) II
shall (modal verb) III
shampoo (n) 8
shape (n) I
she (pron) 1
sheep (n) II
shelter (n) I
shirt (n) II
shock (n) 14
shoe (n) II

shop (v) II
shopper (n) II
shopping (n) 6
short (adj) 4
should (modal v) II
shout (v) 7
show (v) 5
shrink (v) II
sick (adj) 8
sickness (n) 8
side (n) I
sigh (v) 7
sign (n, v) 5, III
silent (adj) III
silk (n) II
silkworm (n) II
similar (adj) 1
simple (adj) 3
simply (adv) I
since (adv) III
sincerely (adv) 1
sing (v) 7
sister (n) 1
situation (n) 14
six (adj) 1
sixteen (adj) 2
sixth (adj) 4
sixty (adj) 3
size (n) I
skin (n) I
skirt (n) II
sky (n) 7
slate (n) 4
sleep (n, v) 13, III
slip (v) 14
slippery (adj) 14
slow (adj, adv) 9
small (adj) 1
smart (adj) III
smell (v) 7
smoke (n) 10
smoke detector (n) 12

snack (n) 13
snow (n) I
so (conj) 1
soap (n) 8
social (adj) 6
soft (adj) 10
soft drink (n) 10
softly (adv) 2
solid (adj) I
solution (n) 7
some (pron, adj) 1
someone (pron) 2
something (pron) 3
sometimes (adv) I
son (n) 1
song (n) 7
sore (adj) 8
sound (n) 7
soup (n) 6
source (n) 12
south (n, adj) I
South America (n) I
South Pole (n) I
space (n) 10
speak (v) 2
special (adj, n) 2, 11
speed (n) 15
spend (v) II
spill (v) 14
spilled (adj) 7
spin (v) II
spinner (n) II
spinning (n) II
spoil (v) 11
sport (n) 3
sports (n pl) 1
spot (n) 5
spring (n) 5
stairs (n pl) 14
stamp (n) 8
stand (v) III
star (n) 5

starchy (adj) 13
start (v) 12
state (n) 1
station (n) III
stay (v) 4
steak (n) 11
steal (v) III
steep (adj) 15
steer (v) 15
step (n, v) 1, 14
stick (n) 5
still (adv) 7
stomach (n) 8
stomachache (n) 8
stop (v) 7
stop sign (n) 5
store (n) 9
story (n) 2
stove (n) 12
straight (adj, adv) I, II
street (n) 1
strong (adj) I
student (n) 1
study (v, n) 2, I
style (n) II
suddenly (adv) 15
sugar (n) 11
suit (n) II
summer (n) 5
sun (n) 5
Sunday (n) 4
super (adj) 11
supermarket (n) 11
sure (adj) II
surplus (n) II
swallow (v) 14
sweater (n) II
sweet (adj, n) 11, 13
swim (v) 6
symbol (n) 5
system (n) 14

T

T-shirt (n) II
table (n) 2
tag (n) II
tailor (n) II
take (v) 2
take back (v) II
take care of (idiom) I
talk (v) 1
tall (adj) I
tape measure (n) II
taste (v) 11
teach (v) 7
teacher (n) 1
teenager (n) II
telephone (n) 2
television (n) 10
tell (v) 1
teller (n) III
temperature (n) 8
temple (n) 6
ten (adj) 1
tennis (n) 3
tenth (adj) 4
term (n) III
test (n) 15
than (adv) I
thank you (int) III
that (conj, pron, adj) 3, 4, 5
the (adj) 1
theater (n) 10
their (adj) 1
them (pron) 1
themselves (pron) 9
then (adv) 2
there (adv) 1
therefore (adv) 8
thermometer (n) 8
these (adj, pron) 1
they (pron) 1
thick (adj) I
thief/thieves (n/n pl) III

thin (adj) 13
thing (n) 1
think (v) 2
third (adj) 4
thirteen (adj) 2
thirty (adj) 3
this (pron, adj) 1
those (adj) 1
thought (v past) 7
thousand (adj) 2
thread (n) II
three (adj) 1
throat (n) 8
through (prep) I
throw (v) 10
Thursday (n) 4
time (n) 3
tip (n) 12
tire (n) 15
title (n) 1
to (prep) 1
today (adv, n) 4
together (adv) I
told (v past) 7
tomorrow (n, adv) 7
tongue (n) 8
too (adv) 1
tool (n) 9
tooth (n) 8
toothache (n) 8
top (n) I
topic (n) III
touch (v) I
town (n) 1
toy (n) 2
tractor (n) 9
tradition (n) 9
traffic (n) 5
train (n) 15
transportation (n) I
travel (n) I
traveler (n) I

tree (n) 7
triangle (n) 15
trip (n) II
trouble (n) 15
truck (n) 15
true (adj) 1
try (v) 6
try on (idiom) II
Tuesday (n) 4
tumble (v) II
turning (n) 12
TV (n) 13
twelfth (adj) 4
twelve (adj) 1
twenty (adj) 2
twice (adv) 8
twin (n) I
twist (v) II
two (adj) 1

U

uncle (n) III
under (prep) 5
underline (v) 2
understand (v) 1
understanding (n) I
understood (v past) 5
unnecessary (adj) 11
unsafe (adj) 14
until (adv, prep) 4
unusual (adj) 5
up (prep, adv) 4
upside-down (adj) 15
us (pron) 2
use (v) 1
used (adj) II
useful (adj) 1
usual (adj) 11
usually (adv) 1

V

vacation (n) III
valuable (adj) 14
value (n) 13
variety (n) I
vegetable (n) 11
vehicle (n) 15
very (adv) 1
video (n) 4
village (n) I
visit (v) 3
vitamin (n) 11
voice (n) 7
volunteer (n, v) 6
vomit (v) 14

W

waist (n) II
wait (v) 7
wake up (v) 12
walk (v, n) I, 6
wall (n) 4
want (v) 3
wardrobe (n) II
warm (adj) I
warn (v) 12
warning (n) 12
was/wasn't (v past) 1, 4
wash (v) II
wash-and-wear (adj) II
washable (adj) II
waste (n) II
watch (v) 4
water (n) I
way (n) 4
we (pron) 1
wear (v) II
weather (n) I
weaver (n) II
Wednesday (n) 4
week (n) 4
weekday (n) 4

weekend (n) 4
weight (n) 13
welcome (adj) 6
well (adv) 5
well-made (adj) II
went (v past) 5
were (v past) 1
west (n, adj) I
wet (adj) I
what (pron) 1
when (adv) 4
where (adv) 2
which (adj, pron) 2, 3
whisper (v) 2
white (adj) 5
who (pron) 1
whole (adj) 1
whose (pron) 1
why (adv) 1
wide (adj) 10
wife (n) 1
will (modal verb) 2
willing (adj) 9
willingness (n) 9
wind (n) 14
window (n) 12
winter (n) 4
wire (n) 12
wisdom (n) 7
wise (adj) 5
wisely (adv) 11
with (prep) 1
without (prep) 5
woman/women (n/n pl) 1
wonderful (adj) 7
wood (n) 9
wool (n) II
word (n) 1
work (v, n) 2
worker (n) 9
world (n) 1
worm (n) II

worry (v) 7
would (modal verb) 9
wring (v) II
write (v) 1
writing (n) 4
written (adj) 15
wrong (adj) 5
wrote (v past) 4

Y

yard (n) 10
year (n) 1
yellow (adj) 5
yes (int) I
yesterday (n) 7
yet (conj) 6
yield (v) 15
yogurt (n) 13
you (pron) 1
young (adj) 3
your (adj) 1
yours (pron) 1
yourself (pron) 1

Z

zip code (n) 1